Foreword by Jack Canfield
Co-creator of the New York Times #1 best-selling series,
Chicken Soup for the Soul®

The
Feel Good
Guide
to
Prosperity

EVA GREGORY

PRAISE FOR THE FEEL GOOD GUIDE TO

"What intrigued me the most about The Feel Good Guide to Prosperity is how Eva weaves together inspirational stories, coaching, and foundational information. It's not so much of a "how to" book, as it is a book whose purpose is to excite the reader into actions that literally, and unequivocally change the reader's life."

-Jack Canfield,
co-creator of the New York Times #1 best-selling series,
Chicken Soup for the Soul®
www.chickensoupforthesoul.com

"A great book contains a magic ingredient; it connects with something inside of you that changes your life ... it makes you want to stretch – go after bigger goals, become a more effective person. Eva's book has affected me that way and I'm sure it will with you. She explains prosperity through the Law of Attraction in a beautiful manner. Every now and then, I am asked what is one of the most important books I have ever read – this is being added to my list."

-Bob Proctor,
Master Success Coach
author of best-selling book *You Were Born Rich*
www.bobproctor.com

"Are you intending to achieve everything that you have been wanting in your life? If you answered yes, then we recommend making The Feel Good Guide to Prosperity one of your essential planning guides. The Feel Good Guide succeeds in presenting powerful ideas and tools for creating a life that is richer, more prosperous, and more enjoyable. Learn to take control of your life and prosperity from the inside, creating greater inner balance as you attract more of what you desire."

-Stacey Hall and Jan Brogniez,
co-authors, *Attracting Perfect Customers...The Power of Strategic Synchronicity*
www.perfectcustomers.com

"Eva Gregory has succeeded in demonstrating how we can truly take control of our own prosperity and experiences of life. Written with lightness, simplicity and enthusiasm, The Feel Good Guide to Prosperity is a valuable tool to help make our journey to prosperity be a rich and rewarding experience. It paves the way for positive inner change that results in positive outer experiences."

-Hale Dwoskin,
author of the New York Times Best Seller *The Sedona Method: Your Key to Lasting Happiness, Success, Peace and Emotional Well-Being*
www.sedonamethod.com

"Finally! Someone has finally made the connection between how we feel and prosperity. Finally! Someone has clearly articulated how we can harness the power of the Law of Attraction to pull prosperity into our lives. Importantly, Eva Gregory has expanded "prosperity" to include a richness in life that makes financial independence a meaningful and joyous experience. I tore through the book with a big smile on my face. A real gem, Eva."

-David Dibble,
Author of *The New Agreements in the Workplace – Releasing the Human Spirit*
www.thenewagreements.com

"Between birth and death, what shall we do? How shall we live? If you have a longing for 'the freedom of wealth, time, health and spirituality', then I urge you to read this marvelous book by Eva Gregory. It will inspire you to create a life worthy of the miracle that is life."

-Robert Rabbin,
author of *Igniting the Soul at Work*
www.robrabbin.com

"I have never seen anyone lay out the logic of the Laws of Attraction and manifestation so clearly as Eva has in the Feel Good Guide to Prosperity. Even the most stubborn skeptics will be drawn to these simple truths. I am sure it will have a profound effect on many people's lives. And the Coach's Corner feature is great. This is a book that asks for the reader's commitment to themselves, and then shows them step by step how to manifest what they desire. What a great work."

-Allan Hardman, Toltec Master
www.joydancer.com

"I find the The Feel Good Guide To Prosperity very inspiring and empowering. I know this book will bring peace and prosperity to many people."

-Bijan,
author of *Absolutely Effortless Prosperity*
www.effortlessprosperity.com

"I love this! It's clear, easy, fun, and -- it works!"

- Joe Vitale,
best-selling author of *Spiritual Marketing*
www.mrfire.com

"A work of art, as inspirational as it is helpful! Eva's written a handbook for everyone, from beginners to old souls, to remind us all how to win at the game of life."

-Mike Dooley,
author of *Notes from the Universe*
and founder of TUT's Adventurers Club
www.tut.com

ALSO BY EVA GREGORY

Daily Pearls of Wisdom (Xlibris Corporation, 2002)

The Feel Good Guide to

EVA GREGORY
foreword by Jack Canfield

Prosperity

Leading Edge Publishers
SAN FRANCISCO

www.feelgoodguidetoprosperity.com
www.abundanceabounds.com

The Feel Good Guide to Prosperity

 Leading Edge Publishers

Copyright © 2004 Printed in the U.S.A.

First edition, December 2004

ISBN: 0-9753027-1-X
Library of Congress Control Number: 2004095078

Acknowledgements

I am thrilled to have this opportunity to acknowledge all the wonderful people who have supported me in my personal life as well as my professional life; who have touched my heart and made a positive impact on me over the years - all of which have culminated in the creation of this book.

I don't want to leave out a single soul. For those of you I haven't thanked individually here, I am more deeply grateful than you will ever know. I thank each and every one of you for your support.

I owe a tremendous amount of thanks to my writing partner, Kim Green-Spangler. I so appreciate you and your God-given talents. This book would absolutely not exist without you.

I am deeply grateful to Sid Smith whose collaboration, encouragement, creative juices and input took the book from a mass of information to a cohesive focus.

To Susan Johnson, artiste extraordinaire, for creating yet another masterpiece in the formatting and design of this book, I appreciate you! You continue to amaze me with your brilliance and talent.

I am forever grateful to my powerhouse of an assistant, Julie Tiffee, who's organizational and administrative skills allow me to charge ahead in my business and endeavors (much of the time like the proverbial 'bull in a china shop') while she masterfully and skillfully juggles the balls I constantly throw in the air.

To Jon Kip, my web guru, I bow down to you…that is when I'm not rolling on the floor splitting my sides laughing from your antics! You are truly a man of many talents. It's amazing how you always give me exactly what I want – even when others say it can't be done. You know how to work your magic! Thanks for being a light in my life.

Thank you, Scott Johnson, for so generously allowing me to use your uplifting music in my audio version of the book. It is refreshing to enjoy music that is so inspiring and empowering.

To Jack Canfield, I can't tell you what it means to me to have had you write the foreword to this book. You're a refreshing example of just how big-hearted, loving and authentic one can be no matter how successful and busy they become.

To my other mentors, including Bob Proctor, Jim Rohn, Robert Allen, Mark Victor Hansen, and Brian Tracy, I continue to eagerly and enthusiastically soak up your wisdom.

To my soul sister and business partner, Jeanna Beanna (that's Jeanna Gabellini to the rest of you), what an adventure we've been on together. Can't wait to see what the Universe has in store for us next! I love you, sista!

To Mary "Mary Extraordinary" Allen, I cherish the years we've had sharing, supporting and holding the focus for each other's successes. You are an inspiration.

To my success partner, colleague and friend, Laura Hess, I'm so thankful the Universe brought our paths together...again!

To Kimberly Barrett, Leta Beam, Mandy Birks, Aaryn Herridge, Loryn Herridge, Adee Horn, Michelle Humphries, Michelle Lisenbury Christensen, Jenny MacCutcheon, Nancy Montier, Jenn Moseley, Joyce Nuss, Lisa Rowan, Kimberly Simon, Noelle Sharp, Mai Vu, Jenn Walker, Dr. Jan Westdorf, Dory Willer, Veronica Yates and all the other Divas in my masterminds, your energy, love and support has been and continues to be my rock.

To a phenomenal woman, Cristina Gavin, I can't tell you how thrilled I am our paths crossed and how much our hours upon hours of questions and discussion about the Universal Laws of Attraction, the curiosity, discoveries, breakthroughs, and yes, even the contrast and challenges in which our explorations have gone, has meant to me. You are truly a Star!

To Annabelle Cooper, Mary Sickel and Sarah Newton, thank you for your willingness to share yourselves and your journey as part of this book.

To all my clients past and present, I have learned and continue to learn so much from you. You've been a catalyst for me reaching new heights in my own life. I appreciate each and every one of you for your part in inspiring this book.

To my first coach, Rich Fettke, through whom I discovered the coaching profession. I will always be grateful for your undying support, encouragement and guidance in helping me spread my wings as a new coach. You will always hold a special place in my heart.

I am especially grateful to my two leading men. To my son, Jeffrey, I love you beyond all boundaries and more. You are the epitome of love and your light shines bright. To my friend, lover and soul mate, Robin Retallick, thank you for being by my side for the ride over the past twenty years. It is Law of Attraction and co-creation at its best! I love you madly.

And finally, to Abraham, Jerry and Esther Hicks. You rock my life! You rock the planet! What am I saying? You rock the Universe! Always and forever, 'there is great love here for you'. May we never be complete.

*This book is dedicated
to the light of my life, my son, Jeffrey
and to the love of my life, Robin*

Table of Contents

FOREWORD

by Jack Canfield

Foreword by JACK CANFIELD

*W*hen I was invited to be on The Jeanna and Eva Show, I never suspected what I was in for. Their energy was so infectious, so delightfully vibrant that I called after the show to jokingly ask what they were taking. What I found was the real deal – two women with a passion for life and a commitment to universal prosperity. I told them I wanted to get to know them better because being on their show was fun, and I want a lot of that kind of high energy fun in my life.

I get a lot of requests from people to either co-author a book with them, or as in this case write a foreword to a book. As with my friendships, I don't take these requests lightly, so there are few that get my attention or time. Not only am I excited about co-authoring a new Chicken Soup for the Soul® book with Eva and Jeanna, I am thrilled to share Eva directly with the world through this book.

I've built my life around collecting and sharing stories. People learn and grow through stories. They are the fabric of the world we live in and the foundation of our relationships. For example, Chicken Soup for the Soul, the book series I co-authored with Mark Victor Hansen, currently has over seventy-three books in print, with over seven thousand stories. We all need to hear stories about success and about overcoming seemingly great odds to find joy and prosperity in our own lives. These stories give us the framework for possibility and abundance that we sometimes can't see from where we're standing. The simple fact is that people love these stories and they make a difference in their lives.

I believe the Universe to be an abundant place, and within each of us is the capacity to achieve great things – true prosperity. Prosperity isn't just about money, but involves the whole of our being. We can have prosperous relationships and prosperous health. We can see, taste, touch and experience prosperity every day. I have said that everything you want is out there waiting for you to ask. Everything you want also wants you. But you have to take action to get it.

In this book, The Feel Good Guide to Prosperity, Eva lays out for you the Laws of Attraction. One premise of the Chicken Soup for the Soul series is that when you're nice to people, they want to be nice back to you. The same is true of every aspect of the Universe. When you're nice to the Universe it wants to be nice back to you. But, like I said, you have to take action to get it.

What intrigued me the most about The Feel Good Guide to Prosperity is how Eva weaves together inspirational stories, coaching, and foundational information. It's not so much of a "how to" book, as it is a book whose purpose is to excite the reader into actions that literally, and unequivocally change the reader's life. Just as I was excited by Eva's enthusiasm and passion, I hope that you will be inspired and excited as you read this book. Everything Eva tells you about the Laws of Attraction matches my own personal experience of how things work.

You can get what you want, and as I've suggested in the story of Markita Andrews, who has sold over 42,000 Girl Scout cookies, it does take courage to ask for what you want. The good news is that the more you ask, the easier (and more fun) it gets. Ask for everything you want. Then keep asking, and asking, and asking. If you never give up, and follow the guidelines in this book, not only will you become more prosperous in every area of your life, you will enjoy every minute of the journey to getting there.

Jack Canfield
Co-author of the New York Times #1 best-selling series, *Chicken Soup for the Soul*® and *The Power of Focus*

CHAPTER 1

The Laws of Attraction

"The only thing standing between you
and your dream is your belief that it is possible
and your willingness to go after it." --Eva

CHAPTER ONE: *The Laws of Attraction*

The Universal Law of Attraction

*A*re you aware of what a powerful creator you are? Do you know that everything that is happening to you or has ever happened to you is, without exception, in full response to your thoughts - and more importantly - the emotions behind those thoughts?

Take a look at your life. There are probably some areas you're really happy with and some areas you're not so happy with. You may even believe you are a victim of your circumstances. I'm here to tell you, you are not a victim! It's simply a matter of understanding how to play the Game (of Life) by understanding the rules...the Laws that define the Game.

Would you agree that whether you believe in the law of gravity or not, it exists? It is the same with Universal Laws. They exist and affect you whether you are aware of them or not. Universal Laws are infinite and beyond all boundaries.

Of all the Laws, the single most powerful Law is the Law of Attraction, which simply states, "Like attracts like". This means that what you are focused on, you draw to you.

Here's how it works. When you are focused on what you want, you are attracting to you what you want. When you are focused on what you do not want, you are attracting to you what you do not want.

Okay, I can sense you rumbling out there and your thoughts are probably going something like, "So if it's that simple and clear, why haven't I known this before?" Or, "I've been focused on money for years, so why don't I have any?"

The Law is simple and clear. However, our thoughts are usually very unfocused and running in many directions at once. For example, you may say, "I want a loving relationship." In that moment, the Universe is orchestrating circumstances and events to bring it to you. And yet in the same sentence, you may sabotage yourself by saying something like, "I feel so alone." So, in essence, the Universal forces say, "Wait a minute. Now he says he feels so alone." And you stop the energy flow.

"I had been studying the manifestation process for years, and I was really searching for more clarity. I was feeling kind of incomplete, even though I have consciously manifested several events in my life. I did not have a clear picture of how creative visualization really worked. All the information I had received so far was very good and helped me a great deal but it felt limited. The skeptic in me said, "I can create the life that I want, but..."

I started thinking about the word "deliberate". I had heard of something called "deliberate creation", so I went on the internet and typed those words into the search engine. Tons of web sites came up. I looked into lots of them, and then one day, Abraham- Hicks.com showed up, and that was it for me.

I listened to my first tape and it was love at first hearing. For the first time I completely and clearly understood the Law of Attraction, how it worked, what it meant. None of this was new information to me, it was just a confirmation of a fact that I had suspected for a long time: "creative power is mine", "I can be, do, have all I desire, no limits". The day that my understanding of the Law of Attraction became clear, I felt free!"
~Annabelle

So, take it a step further. When you are thinking about wanting a new relationship, but feeling so alone, where are your emotions? They are focused in feelings of lack; feelings that you want something you do not believe you can have. Can you see how, by not understanding this Law, we hold things away from us we could otherwise have? Our thoughts and emotions are our attraction base.

Let's take the example of money. You say you've been wanting more money for as long as you can remember. When you think of wanting more money, how do you feel about it? Happy? Elated? Or frustrated? Angry? Sad? Maybe jealous of those who do have money? In my experience, this particular subject has more people on an emotional roller coaster than all other subjects combined. The good news is that it doesn't matter how long you've felt this way or how deeply. You can literally turn it around, and begin flowing money to you by consciously and deliberately practicing the Law of Attraction through your thoughts and feelings.

*"I have to say that when I first heard about the Law
of Attraction, I was on the road to success, but
single and stressed out."*
~Jeanna

Anything in your life you want to change, you can, simply by understanding the Law of Attraction and choosing to deliberately change your thoughts and constantly reach for the thought that feels better. The way you predominantly feel about any given subject is your barometer for knowing what your balance of thought is on that subject. The circumstances of your life are another indicator. If you're ever wondering which end of the barometer your thoughts are

on, check in with your emotions. Your emotions never lie about the way you are flowing your energy.

Coach's Corner

Begin playing with the Law of Attraction.

(Be sure to keep a journal by your side as you read through this book. You'll be taking action all along the way!)

Choose a thought pattern or area of your life you'd like to change. Set your intent and write it down in your journal. Consciously and deliberately offer thoughts about what you want and why you want it. Get into the feeling place of having it and enjoy the visualization as if it's already here. Check in with your emotions to determine how you're flowing your energy around it. If you're feeling less than joyful about it, reach for a thought that feels better. Understand that you are flexing a muscle that in time gets easier and easier. Most importantly, keep it light, make it a game and have fun with it!

NOTE: For more in-depth knowledge of the Law of Attraction I strongly recommend you visit www.abraham-hicks.com (and be sure to tell them Eva sent you!)

The Universal Law of Deliberate Creation

*I*nfinite growth. Eternal change. Never-ending creation. It all begins with thought. Literally, every thought you have influences what you are experiencing. Yet most people's lives change very little. How do you account for that? In the previous section, I said that you can deliberately choose to change your thoughts.

I had a client say to me, "I don't understand, Eva. You're telling me I'm the creator of my experience, and there's no way I would have created this crisis in my life on purpose!" I agree! Certainly not on purpose. Definitely by default. It is the lack of understanding of Universal Laws that has us creating our lives by default. Once you understand these Laws, you can begin to create what you want in your life consciously and deliberately.

> *"Your life may have been a certain way until now,*
> *yet it doesn't have to stay that way. Your life can be*
> *the way you want it beginning NOW. You have the*
> *power to make it different. Make the decision to have*
> *the life you want and do it NOW! "*
> ~Eva

When things are going wrong in our lives, we want to deny any responsibility for creating it. Yet, until you understand the power you hold and accept responsibility for everything in your life -- the good, the bad and the ugly -- you deny your true freedom in life! You are held hostage by the wants and desires and expectations of others. I've got news for you. There is no way possible to satisfy all the wants, desires, and expectations others project on you. It is a losing situation!

Simply put, the Law of Attraction means whatever you focus on you draw to you. So, if you are focused on something you do not want, you attract more of that to you. If you are focused on something you do want, you attract more of that to you. As thinking, feeling human beings we are in a constant mode of creating, whether we believe it or not.

"When I first heard about the Law of Attraction,
I thought I needed to get it all together or everything
would fall apart. I saw myself as someone who knew she
had great potential, so why the heck was I struggling?

Then, things were set in motion for me when I realized
how the Laws gave me permission to follow my internal
beliefs. I always trusted the Laws, but only practiced
using the Laws SOMETIMES!
I became on a mission to deliberately use the
Laws for everything, and this helped me
to become consistent."
~Jeanna

We are creators. Anything you focus on, by Law of Attraction, you create, without exception. Your creativity never stops. The good news is once you understand the Law of Attraction, you can be deliberate in your intent. You can choose thoughts about the experiences and things you do want in your life rather than thinking thoughts about what you don't want in your life. In other words, you begin to create what you want purposefully and intentionally.

The Law of Deliberate Creation is simply understanding the Law of Attraction and then consciously and deliberately choosing the thoughts and emotions that feel better. Always reach for the thought that feels better. How do you

know when you're in alignment with what you want or when you're not? Check in with your emotions. Your emotions never lie!

You may ask, "Where does action come in"? Clearly, as humans, we are action-oriented beings. Yet, when we put our focus on being in action first -- being in the 'doing' first -- we are going about our creative process backwards. The natural order is to identify how you want to feel, then identify what you want from that feeling place. From that point, you will be inspired to the right action.

Let's look at an example. One of my clients wanted to increase her chiropractic business by 30 new clients per month. When we first began the process, both of us were caught up in the tactics, the goals and the how-to's of making it happen. It really got bogged down. (Yes, even I still slip up after all these years. Dang!)

Once I realized what was going on -- trying to make something happen before getting into alignment with it emotionally -- I checked in with her. "Donna, how does this plan feel to you?" There was an enormous amount of resistance, feelings of "should" and the feeling of having to take it all on herself. We tossed it all out the window and began again with what felt good to her.

I sent her away to do absolutely nothing over the next week except get into the feeling place of what it would be like to have 30 new clients coming in every month easily and effortlessly. She journaled and visualized what a day would feel like if clients just flowed to her. She saw them appreciating her and getting the relief they were looking for. She got into the feeling place of what it would be like to have the day-to-day administration handled without her having to be involved and having it be streamlined.

From there, the inspired ideas came for the action steps that worked for her. She went to a class about a database software package that would streamline the administrative side of the business. She organized a newsletter to go out regularly and follow-up letters to be sent to prospects and past clients offering a special just for them. She even found someone else to handle it all so she could be home with her children to enjoy the planning and preparations for their Christmas holiday. Within a month, she was attracting 30 clients a month and working less in the process.

> *"There is no ending. There is always more. Every moment is a new beginning, and a movement beyond what was. An ending of something is nothing more than a new beginning that is unfolding. By focusing on what is coming, you launch new intentions that draw more new experiences to you."*
> ~Eva

One of my favorite quotes from Abraham-Hicks is, "Nothing is more important than that you feel good!" And from that feel-good place, you can easily create all you are wanting in your life. It is the difference between coming from a negative place, working really hard to fix what is wrong -- to being in a positive place, clear about what you want and attracting it to you easily, effortlessly and joyfully.

Most of us haven't quite gotten it yet that life is supposed to be fun! Here you are in this creative playground called 'your life'. It is your job to create what you want in your imagination and get into the feeling place of it already happening. Then allow the Universe to bring about the people, places, circumstances, events and action from inspiration that allow it to become a part of your physical reality.

Coach's Corner

Continue to play with the Law of Attraction.

Remember that area of your life you selected in the first section? You know, the one you set your intention toward?

What would it feel like to have that be exceptionally easy and fun? Right now is the best time to practice having a relaxed mind, which is an essential part of deliberate creation.

Did you know studies have shown perpetually "lucky" people are generally more relaxed about life? Take a little break and relax into your vision of having what you want. No stress. No fuss. Just simple relaxation and ease. How do you feel?

Once in this relaxed place, write down in your journal any ideas, thoughts, or actions that come to mind. Then, *get out there and do them!!* Go talk to people, relax and have fun with others, and see what "chance" encounters happen.

The Universal Law of Allowing

*D*o you think that if someone with beliefs opposed to yours gets their way, you can't have your way? Or do you believe there's room for it all?

Of the three Universal Laws of Attraction, the Law of Allowing is where the rubber meets the road.

Once you begin to understand the concepts of the Law of Attraction and Law of Deliberate Creation, the Universe is ready to grant you your intentions. The question is... are you ready to allow this to happen? The answer depends on the focus of your attention.

The truth is, there is freedom in allowing circumstances to be what they are and people to be who they are, whether you agree with them or not. Really. Even when it comes to poverty, war or disease.

> *"There is freedom in allowing others to be who they are, even as you choose to make changes within yourself."*
> ~Eva

So, how in the world do you accept situations and people that stand for something you don't? Or that want the opposite of what you want? We tend to think we can't have it both ways. So what do we do? We push back! We hold protest marches against war, we organize campaigns against drugs, and we battle disease.

And yet, understanding the Law of Attraction -- that whatever you are focused on you attract more of -- when you are focused on what you do not want in an effort to defeat it or

resist it, you are not allowing what you do want to flow to you.

Remember the Coach's Corner exercise I asked you to do in the previous section? The Law of Allowing is about relaxing – having a relaxed, but positively focused mind – and allowing the Universe to deliver to you what you want.

"First as a coach, I took a class in 'attraction' and learned the power of the process of attracting versus working so hard to get what I need and want. However, I didn't really get it into my bones until I took Eva's course called The Prosperity Game, and I have been shifting my life since then.

Initially I was taking entirely too much time and effort to do anything. After learning about The Laws of Attraction in coaching, big shifts happened in many parts of my life. However my business was still stunted, until I learned from Eva how to simply allow attraction to work in my life."
~Mary

When you say yes to something, you attract more of it into your life, because that is what you are focused on. When you say no to something, you attract more of that into your life, because that is what you are focused on. So in order to allow what you want to flow to you, you must allow others to focus on what they want - even if you don't agree with it.

*There's no reason to wait until the rest of the world
is balanced to achieve balance and
fulfillment in your own life. Only YOU need to
understand what you know for you to have what
you want in your life."*
~Eva

In other words, be more consciously selective about where you choose to focus your attention. Rather than going into resistance about something you don't want or don't agree with, flip your thoughts around to what you do want and make 'Just Say Yes!' your slogan.

Allow what you want to come to you by yes'ing your way through life. 'Just Say Yes' to abundance. 'Just Say Yes' to great relationships. 'Just Say Yes' to a healthy body. 'Just Say Yes' to work that you love. Get the picture? Your job is to simply identify what you want, get into the feeling place of having it and then allow it to flow to you by holding your focus there.

When you understand these principles and put them to use consciously, intentionally and deliberately, you put yourself in a place of non-resistance. How do you know if you're allowing? By noticing how you feel. Your emotions are always your guide. Whenever you are in a place of feeling good, you are in a place of allowing. Nothing is more important than that you feel good!

Coach's Corner

Take an inventory of what you are and are not allowing in your life right now.

A fun and easy way to do this is to notice something just for fun over the next 24 hours.

Notice how many coins you find on the street, in your house, your pockets, or just waiting for you to find them. Pick up all pennies, nickels, dimes, and even $20 bills if you find them.

Then, at the end of the day, see how much loose pocket change you accumulated. Do the same thing for five days in a row. What do you notice as you focus more and more on allowing (relaxed mind!!) things to come to you?

The Science of a Positive Attitude

A Native American elder once described his own inner strug-
gles in this manner: "Inside of me there are two dogs. One of
the dogs is mean and evil. The other dog is good. The mean dog
fights all the time." When asked which dog wins he reflected for
a moment and replied, "The one I feed the most."
– George Bernard Shaw

*Q*uantum physicists have been playing with the notion that our thoughts and feelings have a direct influence on the physical world. Everything, they say, is connected through energy. You know already about the three Laws of Attraction, and how much your thoughts and feelings have to do with what you create in your life. Did you know that scientists are now agreeing with what we call the Laws of Attraction? They are!

Here's a simplified explanation of this scientific phenomena we call the Law of Attraction:

1. At the sub-atomic level, everything is always in motion. Time and space don't exist as we know them. A butterfly merrily flapping its wings in Japan can affect the weather in New York. It's all energy that interacts simultaneously.

2. Thoughts and feelings are also energy. They have been measured as such.

3. Because thoughts and feelings are energy, they vibrate (move). Each thought and feeling vibrates at a specific frequency (how fast it vibrates). Negative feelings vibrate at a slower frequency than positive feelings.

4. The power (amplitude) of the thought or feeling is affected by the strength of the thought or feeling, which in turn is impacted by the number of times that thought or feeling is focused on. That is, if you keep repeating, "money corrupts", it amplifies the vibration of that thought.

With me so far?

Remember, everything is energy, and all energy vibrates at a specific characteristic frequency.

The scientific Law of Attraction states that an object, physical object, thought or feeling, will naturally attract that with which it is in vibrational harmony. Strike a tuning fork, and the strings that are in tune with that vibrating object will also begin to vibrate. Thoughts, ideas, and emotions must follow this Law of Attraction because they too are "objects" with an energetic vibration.

Now we get to the fun part. I suspect by now you really understand the Law of Attraction – like attracts like. Like thoughts or feelings attract thoughts and feelings that are vibrating at the same or similar frequencies. Likewise, these thoughts and feelings attract physical objects such as people and events that are vibrating at a similar frequency.

> *"Your power is in your thoughts. Your job is to dream what you want into being and then, only then, take whatever action you are inspired to take; whatever action you enjoy taking, to make your dream a reality."*
> *~ Eva*

But, how does our mind actually take all this in and process it?

Your brain is assaulted by thousands of messages each second. Everything you see, hear, smell, feel and touch is a message entering your brain.

Part of your brain filters through all these messages and decides which ones will move into your conscious awareness. Have you ever purchased a new car, only to see many of that same car and color on the road for the next week? How about when two people can go to a movie and have entirely different experiences? If you've ever experienced that, you know what I mean by the brain's filtering mechanism.

When you focus your attention on something you don't want, for example, "I don't want to lose any more money!", you're telling your brain to flag anything related to losing money as important. You "see" more evidence to support exactly what you do NOT want to see! It flags it as important because it's what you're focused on.

Scientists say the brain is plastic: it can and does remodel itself, sometimes within a remarkably short period of time. And with the brain, timing is everything. What this means for you is as you focus more of your attention on positive thoughts, you are actually shifting the neural pathways of your brain!

This is why it gets easier as you practice shifting your focus and practicing positive thoughts! Your brain is actually "reprogramming" itself to notice more positive things. Cool, huh?

This is particularly interesting when you think about the impact it can have on our ability to succeed at something. If you're focused on the "bad dog" - that is, why you're failing - you'll strengthen those neural pathways. Conversely,

a continual focus on the "good dog" - success, with a positive mental attitude - strengthens the neural pathways for success!

Coach's Corner

Rather than take my word for it, try a simple experiment for yourself and monitor the results. Pick a color you enjoy seeing. Think about it intently, and with great pleasure for several minutes. Then, notice how often that color shows up during the day, or even how it might be mentioned by others. Go ahead... try it! This is a great way to experience the Laws of Attraction at work!

Manifesting What You Want

*O*kay, so we've talked about the Laws of Attraction and the science behind the Laws. But why should this interest you unless there was a purpose to understanding the Laws of Attraction? I'm guessing you just may be interested in manifesting certain things in your life that either don't currently exist, or don't exist exactly as you want them. Let's explore this idea of manifesting.

What does it mean 'to manifest'? What was the first thing that popped into your mind? Was it 'to create, to come to be, to bring to reality?'

Close. The definition is: 'clearly apparent to the sight or understanding!' Did you know an infinite number of things are manifested every day? That's right! Each thought, each vibration, each feeling or belief manifests a response, be it positive or negative.

> *"Dare to challenge every limiting belief about your-self and watch the true unlimited you reveal itself."*
> ~Eva

One of the most powerful things to understand about man-ifestation is what comes to be in your life began with a thought, feeling or action by you. Compelling, isn't it?

The wonderful person you met, the great new job with full benefits, or the perfect house with all of that closet space and the finished basement, all began with your thoughts. Did you pat yourself on the back? Go ahead. Please give credit where it is due!

On the other hand, the lack of funds, marital break-up, or

business standstill is also of your making. How does one harness this powerful tool to create the things that are wanted, instead of the things that aren't?

"My life was good. I was married to a man I love and who loves me. I was the mother of a wonderful boy; I had made most of my dreams come true, but I was feeling the ups and downs of world events. My mood was dictated by what was happening outside me.

Dreams do come true and we can manifest all we want but how do we sustain them. How do we keep them? I knew a lot about metaphysics, but I still felt powerless, like the ultimate decision was not mine. I had replaced God in the sky with God within, but "I" was not in the picture when it came to who has the creative control in my life.

I was happy but hungry for more. I read every book on the matter of manifestation, but they had the same information. I was not moving forward and I could feel it. I even went back to old habits like getting involved in gossip chats at the office, feeling down on Sunday afternoons because I had to go back to work the next day, being fearful of the future, etc. My old house felt crowded and no longer comfortable, AAGHH! I was stuck!!! Big time!!!"
~Annabelle

The answer is by becoming more in tune with your thoughts, feelings, situations, and actions. The more aware you are of where your thoughts are wandering, the more control you will have over what is being manifested.

Ben is one of a growing number of work-from-home dads. It is his responsibility to take care of two children under the

age of four each day, while running his successful web design business. Is it challenging? Absolutely, but Ben has managed quite nicely by making manifestation work for him. His sons used to pick the most inopportune time to make noise, wreak havoc, and well...act like toddlers! But now this rarely occurs because Ben takes the time throughout his day to focus his thoughts on what actions he would like to see occur: quiet play, easy nap-time routines, and uneventful meals, and it works! No longer does Ben have to hide in the bathroom to take important business calls. He has effectively managed to create the work environment he needs.

Ben is taking full responsibility for his thoughts and for what then manifests in his life as a result of his thoughts!

Make more decisions about what you want in every day. Each time you make a decision, you become a filter that clarifies what you want, and the Universe begins flowing situations, circumstances and people towards its manifestation.

Manifestation requires time, patience and practice. It can be difficult to change bad habits and to train yourself to think differently, and it is so rewarding when the effort is made. So begin manifesting the things you want by making that mental shift.

> *"Make more decisions about what you want in every day. Each time you make a decision, you become a filter that clarifies what you want, and the Universe begins flowing situations, circumstances and people towards it manifestations."*
> ~Eva

Coach's Corner

Start small if you have to, but start today. Focus on what you want, instead of what you don't have, always keeping your eyes on the goal. Remember to look for and appreciate what is manifesting. You just have to identify them as what you asked for, so be careful what you ask for.

Remember to show gratitude as your dreams and desires appear. Remember, the more gratitude (positive energy) that is shown, the more positive energy will flow back to you. With all of this positive imagery and energy, success will abound. So, start using these tips now. You'll be manifesting a great deal more of what you want. I guarantee you will be impressed by the fruits of your effort.

CHAPTER 2

Your Role in Attraction

"Be more aware in every day about what you think,
which leads to the words you speak, which leads to the
actions you take. Be crystal clear in your intent, for your
habits of thought create your reality." --Eva

Defining Your Dash

*I*f you have ever been to a cemetery, you have probably noticed the straight rows of markers (some fancy, some simple) which testify to lives lived. Each marker bears a name, dates born and passed, and sometimes a loving reference. But a closer look reveals what each and every person had in common. I'm talking of course about the 'dash'.

That dash represents what they chose to do with their lives between those two vital dates.

> *"If the world is our playground, why aren't we playing more?"*
> ~Eva

What occurs to me -- what startles me -- is that while I will choose neither the date of my birth nor the date of my death, I and I alone will be responsible for defining my dash. While this list is not comprehensive, I hope it will be a good starting point for questions only you are qualified to ask yourself.

1. Do you live in integrity? While integrity has been defined in many ways, I believe it can best be defined as the space between your words and your deeds. If you have children, you have been blessed with a live-in integrity meter. Just recently a third grader was sent to the principal's office for cursing. The dutiful principal called the boy's parents and soon the father arrived. On being told what his son had done the father exclaimed, "Where in the #%@* did he learn to speak like that?" Where indeed.

2. Do you live honestly? A further question to ask is "Am

I honest with myself?" When you commit to an honest life, both with yourself and others, you will find a quality of life that simply cannot be purchased with any other currency. You will live cleanly, knowing that you can look others straight in the eye and be yourself.

3.   What do you value? To put a finer point on this, do you value people over things? While having things is fine, it is the people in our lives that enrich it. It is our communication with people, verbal and otherwise, that can help us become more than we ever imagined. And it empowers us to help others discover their true worth as well.

While all of our dashes will be defined differently, I know this one thing for certain. When it comes to defining your dash, *you* are the author. Make it the best dash it can be.

In the next section I'll help you to understand the Laws of Attraction at a deeper level by taking full responsibility for what you have in your life today. This step is essential in manifesting something new. Only by accepting responsibility for where you are can you move deliberately to a new place.

Coach's Corner

Begin creating your own dash.

Review the above list in this section – Integrity, Honesty, and Values - and add to it. Create your own list of qualities that are important to you. Take a moment to review your goals and see how they align with the dash you want for your life.

Review your actions from the past day, week, month -- and see how wide the gap is between your words and your actions. Examine yourself and determine if what you are doing is in harmony with what you really want.

The Law of Use

*D*id you take a moment to review how you're living your "dash"? One thing many of us do is live life as if what we have will be taken from us. Paying attention to your Integrity, Honesty and Values, among other things, also involves a strong element of trust.

We've all heard the phrase "use it or lose it." Doctors and trainers tell us we must exercise our muscles or they will lose the ability to perform and we will grow weak. Our professors tell us to challenge our minds so they will grow strong and we can achieve our goals.

How can we use what we have everyday to ensure we remain strong, able to face life's challenges? By understanding the Law of Use. Simply stated, use what you have today and tomorrow you will have more.

> *"Passion is inspiration at full tilt. In following your passion, you make the impossible possible."*
> ~Eva

Here are two ways to begin harnessing the Law of Use in your life today.

Participate in new ways of thinking. What is the biggest challenge you face today? Define that challenge, then look at it from different points of view. If the challenge involves other people, pretend you are those people and see it from their point of view. Now imagine that you are the only resource available to solve the problem. What will the outcome look like then? What if you did nothing about this challenge? What if all you did for the next week was face this challenge? Imagining all the scenarios will help you see the big picture, stretch your ways of thinking, and help you put things in perspective too.

"When I first started playing with the Law of Attraction, I saw my biggest personal responsibility as learning to dream large again, and to allow the Universe and all its magic to happen around me.

It is surprising how hard this is when you are well over 40 years old. It seems my whole life is being spent getting back to age seven, when everything seemed possible and effortless."
~Mary

Stretch your physical world. Often the routine of our physical world impacts our ability to find creative solutions to challenges we face. Shaking up our physical world a bit can help us gain perspective and open our thinking as well.

⁐ *Coach's Corner*

We can get into such ruts! Practice doing some things a little differently.

Open up your creativity by writing with the opposite hand for one hour today. Make your next meeting a "stand up" meeting where no one sits down. You'll be amazed at how quickly people become very creative.

Other things you can try include driving to work via a different route, putting your shoes on in the opposite order, or closing your eyes as you think. Buy five different kinds of breakfast cereal instead of the usual Raisin Bran or granola. Set your alarm clock ten minutes earlier. Wear something new and different every day for the next week.

When we make these small physical changes, we trigger our minds to look at things in a new way. Not only do we grow, but we learn to see the world from a different point of view. When that happens, we exercise our vision as well as our mind and body.

Begin practicing opening to new ways of doing and seeing things, and see what else opens to you.

Doing My Thing, Minding My Own Business

*O*ne of the challenges we face when we begin doing things differently in our lives is that it upsets the balance those around us feel. It makes them uncomfortable when we change. Isn't that odd? You'd think our friends would celebrate our changes. Some do, but what you may find when you start down a new path is that those around you will rebel, maybe even saying things that are intended to pull you back to the old ways.

"The route to success is persistence."
~Eva

Does worrying about what others think of you or what you are doing cause you anxiety and sleepless nights? Do you tailor your actions or behavior to the opinions of others?

If so, then you are certainly not alone! It seems we're always judging our actions, even our thoughts, by what others may or may not think. The title of a book by Terry Cole Whitaker really struck a cord. The book is entitled "What You Think of Me is None of My Business." Imagine how liberating it would be to adopt this title as your personal motto and put it into practice.

"When I first began soaking up this material, I saw it all as up to me and that felt empowering!"
~Jeanna

Envision yourself looking at the captions on a magazine cover and not caring what the latest expert says is acceptable, fashionable, or tolerable. How about being able to attend this year's holiday parties without caring what colleagues, acquaintances, relatives, or friends are thinking about you?

Can you feel the self-confidence and positive energy that radiates when you make the   decision to let someone else take ownership of their beliefs, ideas or negativity? Phyllis, Julie, and Trevor had to experience it first hand to feel it.

Phyllis, Julie, and Trevor have been friends since childhood. They have mutual friends and work for the same company. They have all experienced the phenomena of letting someone else's hang-ups become their own. They were not looking forward to the holiday season because they knew what kinds of   comments typically awaited them. This year they got together at Thanksgiving and decided they were tired of being victims. They prepared for the holiday festivities with excitement knowing they were going to seize control and they had each other for support.

"Since I had confirmed that I have absolute control over my life, and my thoughts and feelings were basically attracting events and people into my life, then I had to be in control of my emotions. I could not allow feelings and thoughts to run rampant in my mind and I had to stop accepting every thought as the truth.

"Don't believe everything you think" became my motto. I found this sentence in a web site about deliberate creation, loved it and made it mine.

*My role was to make choices: does it feel good or
not? Very simple."*
~Annabelle

When Phyllis arrived at the company Christmas party
alone and immediately ran into a very happily married co-
worker, instead of letting her co-worker's snide comment
about being dateless bother her, she replied that she wel-
comed the opportunity to meet other people and had intentionally come solo. She felt great as she walked away and
left her co-worker fumbling for a retort. How good it felt to
not worry about what someone else thought for a change.
She felt in control and intended to thoroughly enjoy her
evening.

When Julie left the dance floor looking for a cool drink, her
ex-husband walked up to her and remarked that she
looked good despite the extra pounds she had put on.
Instead of becoming self-conscious, Julie told him she was
glad he thought so and that she hadn't felt so good in years.
Just as he was about to say something, someone walked up
to her and asked her to dance. Julie felt great as she danced
off. She stood in her truth and the outcome was fantastic.

Trevor stood back and observed the crowd. He had seen
the exchanges the girls had and he was impressed. He
hoped he could follow through too. He knew his co-workers joked about the fact that he still lived at home at his age,
and he knew the word had leaked into the neighboring
office where Shelby worked. He wanted to ask her out, but
was not sure how receptive she would be. After all, most
men over 30 do not live at home. As he turned to find
Phyllis to ask for advice, he bumped right into Shelby and
had to grab her to keep her from falling! He immediately
apologized and was amazed when she said she was look-

ing for him. He asked her to dance and while they were dancing she told him she still lived at home too! Trevor was so pleased he did not revert to his old ways. Had he paid attention to what his co-workers thought of him, he never would have asked her to dance.

> *"Each of us brings our own uniqueness to this life.*
> *Rather than comparing yourself to others, set your*
> *own standards."*
> ~Eva

The next day, when the three friends got together to reminisce, they had all learned a great deal from their "Coming Out." They learned that being true to themselves was incredibly rewarding. They had not paid attention to the shoulds and ought-to's that typically surrounded them and decided to enjoy their night. They were happy and had much higher self-esteem the next day. They knew they were going to continue living their lives with the new motto firmly in place.

Coach's Corner

Are you being authentic and standing in your truth? Where are you letting others' beliefs and expectations dictate your life? Are you minding someone else's business? If so, isn't it time to start doing your own thing and minding your own business? It's their hang-up, not yours! My challenge to you is to release worrying about what others think of you and be willing to be your true, authentic self. The quality of your life will improve radically!

The Best Relationship Going

*D*o you know the truth I spoke of in the last section? Think about it for a moment. Who is it I am asking you to have a relationship with? Yourself, of course!

February is the month commonly referred to as the "month of love". It is the month in which relationships with others are sought after, discussed or analyzed. Yet, it is our relationship with self that is the most important relationship of all. Is this selfishness? On the contrary, it is the ultimate act of selflessness when the relationship with self is explored, nurtured, and celebrated.

> *"Why settle for just being the star in the play called 'Your Life' when you can be the writer, director and producer as well?"*
> ~Eva

The relationship with self is probably the most ignored or repressed relationship in existence. It is so easy to put others ahead of ourselves, to make others the center of our world, to give others the burden of making our existence a happy one, but it can take a toll on the relationship itself. Take for example the mother who spends all her time caring for her child and takes no time for herself. A lack of downtime will eventually make her irritable, short-tempered and perhaps even resentful of her child. A little time away from the child would provide the mother with a well-deserved chance for rejuvenation. The same can be said for an adult relationship.

It's the understanding, care, and love we demonstrate to ourselves that allows us to be the best person we can be, which establishes a foundation for our relationship with others. The way we view ourselves and nurture ourselves has a direct bearing on the image that is presented to others. People that are confident about their abilities, and comfortable in their own skin with great self-esteem, will send such powerful vibes out into the Universe they will have no problem attracting the right type of people into their lives. Loving yourself first allows others to love you back. Why? Because as we know, like attracts like.

"When I first heard about this Law of Attraction, I initially thought that it was a bunch of hype to make money off me. I really doubted myself. Since it hadn't worked before, there must be something wrong with me.

Something shifted for me when I started to let go and trust God, or the Universe (same thing), and at the same time take care of myself. "
~Mary

Do you have a strong, healthy, positive attitude about yourself? Do you look at yourself as the source for having all your needs met? Do you manage to spend some time each day self-nurturing? If you answered yes to any of these questions, CONGRATULATIONS! You have a very healthy relationship with yourself. If you answered no, that's alright. Not everyone will be able to answer yes right now, but it's just a matter of time.

Here are a few ways one can build a relationship with self that will be a springboard to other relationship successes:

1. **Firstly, give your self-esteem a check.** You deserve to

feel good about yourself. If you don't feel good about you, how can you expect others to?

2. **Secondly, pay attention to your internal dialogue.** Are you in the place that allows you to be honest with yourself in a caring manner? If not, turn off the self-sabotage messages and substitute positive self-talk.

3. **Thirdly, if your outer image is causing a conflict with your inner image, take the action steps that will make you feel better.** A little change on the outside can make a world of difference on the inside.

4. **Next take time for yourself.** Finding daily quiet time or time to pursue your passions is very important. Don't shortchange yourself on the things that have the power to rejuvenate your spirit.

"This discovery that I am actually responsible for creating what happens in my life and understanding the Law of Attraction felt so wonderful and so liberating that several times I asked myself, "have I lost my mind?" "Is this how it feels to go crazy?"

There is a history of mental illness in my family and even while I am writing this I notice the resistance to absolute freedom. But the truth between this knowing and mental illness is that I do have control of my actions and emotions, and there is also the good catholic girl that still thinks that it's blasphemy to think of herself as equal to God.

I have learned to let those issues be what they are. One thing that I love about the Law of Attraction is that we don't have to bother putting issues to rest - we just have to choose a different thought!"
~Annabelle

5. **Lastly, become self-sufficient.** It is wonderful to have people in your life just because you want them to be there, not because you need them to be there. It is your responsibility to take care of you and to make sure your internal and external needs are being met.

Remember, if you want love, you must give love and make sure you are giving love to you in that equation, first and foremost. It's not selfish at all, just very, very, wise.

> *"True self-esteem is based on being okay with your-self, regardless of what you can do or can't do."*
> ~Eva

As you begin paying more attention to yourself, trusting yourself, and taking care of yourself, your attitude about the world will naturally improve. In the next chapter, I'll give you some specific ideas on how you can more consciously and deliberately cultivate a positive attitude that will greatly accelerate the results you get from following the Laws of Attraction.

Coach's Corner

It's time to practice self-love and take full responsibility for your life.

First, do something good for yourself. Right now. I don't care if that means you put this book down and go outside for a walk. Do it. Now.

Ready for the next thing to practice?
Go someplace where there are a number of people. Look around and pick out someone for whom you don't particularly have an affinity, but aren't necessarily repulsed by. That is, someone who feels pretty neutral to you.

Take responsibility for what happens. Imagine whatever you think next has a direct impact on that person's life. Clear your thoughts, and bring your energy into a place of profound appreciation and positive thought.

Then, step back and see what happens.

CHAPTER 3

Developing an Attractive Attitude

"Never under-estimate the power of your attitude.
Maintaining your inner balance and attitude puts
you in the position of making a positive difference
on those around you." -- Eva

What is an Attractive Attitude?

*B*y now I hope you have some sense of the power behind the Laws of Attraction, and how you can take an active role in manifesting exactly what you want.

It's time to amp things up by developing an attractive attitude. Before we talk about an attractive attitude, here's an idea of what I mean by having an un-attractive attitude:

I give up! This sort of thing never works out for me!

Why does the luck always happen to someone else?

If anything can go wrong, it will!

What's there to be thankful for? My life is a mess!

As you've seen, this kind of thinking will just bring you more of the same bad luck and misfortune. We have this notion in our culture that "putting on a happy face" is a bad thing, and that being called "Pollyanna" is a major put-down.

What's wrong with being a Pollyanna? Pollyanna was the orphan girl who brought sunshine and lightness to everyone she met. She was happy, and brought happiness to her entire town. Pollyanna had a very attractive attitude.

Greg held a skeptical view of the world, and especially the management of his company. If anything went wrong, he figured it was because of one of their stupid policies or decisions. His wasn't holding a very attractive attitude – at least he wasn't attracting what he wanted! He kept attract-

ing more things that fed his skepticism and helped him feel even more justified in his attitude about management.

It was really hard for him, but over time he started shifting his attitude from skeptical to hopeful. He looked at each situation as a way to improve his attitude. Instead of focusing on what was wrong, he saw it as an indication he was still a little off target with his feelings and thoughts. He kept recognizing what he didn't want, and asked in each situation what he did want. This gave him a sense of hope, which made him feel better, and in turn made him more attractive to what he really wanted. It took some time, but eventually, he noticed more and more things working well, even though he had the same management team.

> *"To get the best, expect the best."*
> ~Eva

Greg's attitude and expectations changed, and as a result he attracted more of what he wanted. Part of this is awareness of what might already be sitting right in front of him, and part of it is his new ability to attract something new that is in alignment with his attitude.

So, instead of giving up because nothing ever works out for you, start adopting an attractive attitude by being more like Pollyanna. See the world through rose-colored glasses, and you'll see more roses. Choose to persist because you know at some point you will get that "lucky" break, and it will work out.

Coach's Corner

Develop a more attractive attitude.

What's one area of your life that isn't going as well as you would like? Lack of money? A job you don't like? "Unlucky" at love?

Pick one area, and choose to have a positive attitude about it. I'm not saying you should be thrilled you have no money. But, Pollyanna would ask you to see that you now have some valuable information that will help you attract more money. See if you can find 100 things about your current situation that are working.

Write them in your journal and come back to read them when you need a good reminder. Feel better? Good!

Let Your Light Shine Through

In the previous section, Greg changed his attitude and things miraculously shifted around him. Essentially what he was able to do was have his true nature emerge instead of his corporate persona. In our society, so much of who we are is identified by what we do – meaning our job or career. But we've somehow gotten it backwards over the years. It isn't what we do that identifies us, but who we are that's important. The self that is brought to work each morning, that is present in our interactions, and that manages to shine through whether we are poor or Fortune 100 CEO's is the real essence of who we are. It is that essence that can help us make a job or career we do not like into a learning experience and a vehicle for letting our "inner light" shine through.

"Be the type of person you are looking for in life,
and demand that you can be better than you thought
you could be."
~Eva

Each day we hear of people that are very unhappy in their careers, or are experiencing downsizing and lay-offs. Unfortunately it is very common in today's world. While there are many people who complain and feel downtrodden, there are also those that seem to be able to make the best of a bad situation, no matter what. How do they do that? They have a strong sense of self and, typically, a very healthy dose of optimism.

"I have always been a very enthusiastic person but I
never believed it could happen to me. I believed that
you had to struggle and work hard to get what you
wanted in life.

*When I first heard about the Laws of Attraction, I
thought, 'this is just too easy, it cannot work'.
'Things are supposed to be a struggle.'*

*I figured this was a load of rubbish and that if I
spent time doing this nothing would happen, except
that I would end up broke! I thought I may be
worse off than when I started. I thought everyone
owed me something and that I was a victim of circumstances. I was angry with the world and
thought that I did not deserve anything good. I
thought 'yeah, like this will happen to me.'*

*The truth that I connected with was that the outside
world is a reflection of what is inside. I could look
back on my life and see where this had been true."*
~Sarah

They have, in short, a positive attitude about life. Take
George, for instance. George is a cab driver. He was laid off
from his 15-year job with a large company and had to
secure employment immediately to be able to continue to
care for his family. A friend told him about a cab company
that was looking for dependable drivers and George knew
this was the perfect temporary solution for him. So he
applied for the job and began driving the next week.

George does not like driving a cab. He would prefer to be
back in his old office doing the job he loved, but he knows
this is what is needed of him for the moment. George could
be sullen or sarcastic about these life-changing events. He
could be distant, obnoxious, or rude to his customers, but
he isn't. In fact, George has many fares request him by
name! They find him always cheerful and funny. He smiles
and jokes with them as he whisks them to their destina-

tions and inevitably, he is known for his ability to help brighten someone else's day. George has the ability of using his inner light to make a difference in the lives of others.

Everyone can identify qualities in themselves they both like and dislike. Too often we dwell on the areas we feel need improvement and spend barely a nanosecond patting ourselves on the back for things we consider to be good. When was the last time you actually acknowledged those positive inner light qualities within you?

Here is an exercise. Take out a sheet of paper and make a list of those things about yourself you consider good qualities. Once you've made your list, I'd like you to sit back and review how you implement these qualities in your everyday life. I'll bet you will find you either do them automatically or you do not exhibit them nearly enough. In fact, I bet that once you have your list in hand, you will immediately be able to come up with ways you can put them to use.

"When I first started following the Laws of Attraction, my attitude was positive. However, I gave up easily in the beginning because it wasn't a fast process and my old habits wanted to take over.

What helped was seeing that the truth of abundance was actually in alignment with my spiritual beliefs and my faith. They were very synergistic."
~Mary

Your goal is to draw from this bag of "inner light" qualities and have them become the essence of who you are as you apply them to your daily interactions. From this, you will begin to experience a much more positive existence. You will find yourself looking for ways to implement these qualities, learn not to dwell on the negative, and seek out ways to make a difference in your life and the lives of others. It is a way to step out of yourself and learn to love and appreciate the work and life you have, even if they are not what you ultimately desire. In short, it is a way of living in the moment that will produce startling results.

Remember the Law of Attraction? Want to bet when you start exuding energy, lightness, and laughter these same qualities will begin manifesting themselves in your life at a more rapid pace? You already know the answer.

Coach's Corner

Get out your journal and start making a list of those things you consider good quality. While you're at it, why not come up with at least five positive things to say about the job or career you have now? I'll even get you started:

"I appreciate the fact that I have a job that helps me make ends meet."

In case you do not currently have a job, this one's for you:

"I appreciate the fact that I have a well-earned break from the work force."

See how easy that was? Now it's up to you to let that inner light shine through.

Don't Take It Personally!

*S*ometimes it can feel nearly impossible to let your light shine through when it also feels like there is a conspiracy and the whole world is picking on you. Your friends, family, colleagues, even strangers look at you oddly, as if there were a big fat pimple in the middle of your nose. Your feeling is they are really talking about you, even though they are making general statements. Who do they think they're kidding, you ask.

It can even feel like strangers are going out of their way to make your day difficult. You've been bumped with shopping carts and cut off on the road by inconsiderate people. Sound a little familiar?

Here is the question -- is everyone really out to get you, or is it your own baggage that makes you perceive everyone has an agenda with your name on it? This is an important question to consider if you really want to develop an attractive attitude (or an attitude of attraction!).

Could it be possible people are just carrying on with their lives, and the things that are happening are just -- happening? Perhaps people really are speaking in generalities, but are you taking it personally?

What are your thoughts about Glen? Glen is driving home from work in his sleek, low-to-the-ground sports car. He's had an incredibly bad day and cannot wait to get home and relax. He is almost near his exit and needs to merge from the middle lane to get to the off ramp. He puts on his signal, sees an opening and starts to go for it when the person behind him jumps right in. Glen is livid! He calls the person a few well-chosen names and stews about it the rest of

the way home. Glen knows the person behind him did it on purpose. He must have seen Glen's turn signal!

In reality, the person behind Glen did not notice his signal. He was not sure how to reach his destination and asked his wife for directions. At the last minute, she realized their exit was fast approaching and told him to get over right away. He was not out to "get" Glen. He never even saw him. Boy, talk about two different perceptions of the same situation!

"I thought that this was good to be true. I thought "It's impossible that I am this powerful being." "What about bad things that happen to good people", and of course, "This is crazy, life cannot be that simple".

A few events in my life as an example convinced me of the absolute truth of the Law of Attraction.

My concept of myself is like an inner mirror and the physical reality that I become aware of is the reflection of this self-concept. As a child, I felt like a victim and powerless. My second grade teacher agreed with my feeling and let me know it. I did not like myself. She did not like me.

After my younger brother became blind, the emotional vibration in my house was one of grief and anger. The events that followed my brother's illness were a reflection of this. It was one of the saddest years of my life.

Knowing that this was the Law of Attraction at work makes these events logical and erases the grim view I had when I looked back. It made perfect sense."
~Annabelle

Ironically, that week was not a good one for Glen. Earlier in the week, a deer darted out from the woods as he was driving along, bounced off the top of his car, spun around and returned to the woods from where it came. Then, as he was pulling into his driveway after a long day, he heard that all-too-familiar sound of pavement scraping the bottom of his beautiful car. Glen was not having a wonderful week.

Isn't it interesting, though, that in these instances, Glen did not blame the deer or the pavement or swear they were out to "get" him. He wasn't pleased, but he also didn't feel victimized by the pavement or the deer. If someone had even suggested such an idea to Glen, he'd have thought their idea a bit silly. It never occurred to him to take these situations personally, yet he was completely convinced the other driver cut him off intentionally.

Did Glen take it personally because the situation was "caused" by a person, and not an animal or thing? This could be very likely, and if so, Glen could gain a lot by changing his perspective and his attitude.

> *"Your attitude can make you or break you.*
> *You choose."*
> ~Eva

What might a change in perspective accomplish for Glen? For starters, he would not be in a bad mood about being cut off! It might also help him lighten up and relax. It takes a great deal of emotional energy to be angry and defensive. Glen would probably also laugh a little more. When you stop taking things personally, you can see the humor in situations. Wow, a change in perspective could make a dramatic difference in his life. Talk about an attractive attitude! Who wouldn't want to be around a smiling, laughing Glen?

How can you shift your perspective about people who mean no more harm to you than the deer or the pavement did to Glen? The meaning you attach to any situation dramatically effects your attitude, and as you've seen, your attitude impacts what you attract to you. The reasons people do things can be as diverse as the flowers in a field. It can be different for each person.

When something happens over which you have no control, such as the situation with Glen, try exploring a few different perspectives to find the one that generates an attractive attitude. You may ask if you are tolerating or accepting something you shouldn't. Does it really matter? More than likely this is an   isolated incident that, if you let it, can keep on "giving" for the rest of the day. Find the   perspective that will help you shrug it off and not take it personally. You'll be amazed at how simply, by changing perspectives, you can change the quality of your life!

Coach's Corner

What's something that happened recently about which you're still fuming? Something over which you had no control, and seemed to happen to you purposefully. Got it?

Draw a pie with eight slices. Fill each slice with a different perspective about what might have happened. Try each perspective on for size, then sit for a while with the one that gives you the best feeling – the one in which you're not taking the incident as a personal affront. Notice how much your attitude shifts as you take on this new perspective, then keep stepping back into that perspective throughout the day as needed. Take two perspectives and call me in the morning!

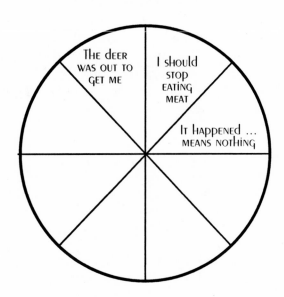

Develop A Magnetic Lifestyle

*E*ach of us possesses the ultimate tool for creating success and attracting the things in life we truly desire. What is the secret? Our positive thoughts. This should not be new to you, considering what I've already said about having a positive attitude. While these positive thoughts are the foundation of having an attractive attitude, it is not always easy to accomplish.

When I suggest having positive thoughts, I often hear a lot of skepticism. Who am I? Peter Pan? All we have to do is "think good thoughts?" But it is entirely true! Our lives are like the proverbial blank canvas, and we hold the paintbrush. In the infamous words of Napoleon Hill, "Anything your mind can conceive and believe, it can achieve." By spending his life studying the most successful people in the world, he discovered this simple truth. It is up to us to visualize and manifest the things we want in life, including money and prosperity. Doesn't it sound easy? Actually, it is, but in order for it to work we need to silence the negative self-talk that tells us our thoughts are crazy or unachievable.

> *"You have the power to create all the abundance you*
> *need. Release your thoughts and feelings of lack.*
> *Trust your own inner wisdom to create all you could*
> *ever need or want in your life."*
> ~Eva

Can it be done? Yes, several well-known millionaires clearly did not listen as both inner and outer voices suggested they may not succeed. Think of Bill Gates, Oprah Winfrey, or Tom Cruise, all self-made millionaires, who ignored the comments, criticisms, and niggling fears and forged ahead toward success.

Are you ready to let go of your fears and start allowing the things in life that you want most?

Let's begin with thoughts. They are powerful energetic forces that create change. When we spend time concentrating on dark thoughts, such as lack, debt, despair, sadness, or bad moods, tangible results of these thoughts surface. When we have positive thoughts that invoke images of growth, awareness, success, and nurturing, the results are favorable. Our minds take us to the places our thoughts lead it to.

For example, try this: focus for a moment on a time in your life when you felt like the happiest person on earth. Can you feel that positive energy radiating from your chest? I'll bet there is a smile on your face, and your mood has improved – considerably, too. Powerful, huh? And that was with a single remembrance. Think of the possibilities if you could create these feelings at will in every aspect of your life.

"When I started thinking about the possibility of having my destiny in my hands in my early twenties, the feeling of being helpless began to shift. I was feeling stronger and bold. I found a job that took me to far away places by myself. I saw myself as smart, fun, and light. Guess what? I traveled, partied, lost weight effortlessly and came in contact with my first metaphysical material.

In earlier years, my mood was one of disappointment. I had been married for six years, but I may as well have been single because I was so lonely and depressed. I had lost myself, and worst of all I had attracted this man using creative visualization. So

*where did I go wrong? Eventually, I was divorced
and scared of being on my own.*

*Looking back I can say that my thoughts and feel-
ings at the time were reflected in every single
event."*
~Annabelle

How can we make this a part of our everyday lives? By
learning how to ask for what you want, and having a positive attitude about what you are requesting. Many of us
speak of wealth and success and can be heard stating "All
you need is a dollar and a dream" when it is time for a big
lottery drawing.

But is that really how you feel about money? Do you think
wealth makes people pretentious, greedy, or overly ambi-
tious? If so, you may be blocking yourself when it comes to
creating wealth for yourself. The positive attitude about
wealth must take place both consciously and unconsciously. Imagine what your life would be like if you attracted
enough wealth to be financially free. You would have time
to spend with your family, pursue hobbies, donate time to
charitable organizations, or anything else you choose. Isn't
that a wonderfully powerful and positive vision? But wait!
Can't you also have a wealth of good friends, family members or activities? What about a wealth of good health?
There are many ways to view wealth. Thinking positively
will help you develop into a wealth magnet, so release your
"wealth hang-ups" along with the power they have to repel
your success.

Changing your habits can seem rather difficult at first, but
with practice, positive thinking and a positive attitude, it
becomes much easier. In fact, as you notice the things that

are showing up from your thoughts, it becomes easier to remember just how much control you have over the things that do materialize on a daily basis.

If you doubt any of this to be true, be sure to re-read the section on the Science of a Positive Attitude in Chapter One. Go back and read whatever you need in order to convince yourself of the truth of positive thinking!

Coach's Corner

Use your journal to track all the things that are shifting and manifesting as you practice the Laws of Attraction. The key is to focus, stay committed, and not beat yourself up if you backslide. You've been thinking one way for many years and it will take some time to change your focus, but you can master positive thinking, develop a positive attitude and attract the things in life you want and deserve.

The Power of Thanks

*O*ne of the best ways to practice positive, attractive thinking is through words of gratitude. Words are powerful things. From ancient times until today, scholars and wise people have believed words contain power.

The words we choose do have power, and they reflect a good deal of what is going on inside us. Whether you express thanks a hundred times a day, or haven't let these words pass through your lips in quite some time, the fact is the power of thanks can change your world today.

"I thought I was here to change the world. I found I was here to change myself."
~Eva

Thanks Changes Us

When we have a heartfelt attitude of thankfulness, greed and all that goes with it go out the door. It's just not possible for greed, envy, bitterness, jealousy, and all those other nasties that attempt to invade our brain, to live in a heart full of gratitude.

People often attempt to change and grow by shedding old, bad habits. While a focus on what you want to change is good, the fastest way to achieve that change is to replace bad thoughts and attitudes with good. Ask yourself what you have to be thankful for today. Keep your focus in the now. Can you walk? Can you read? Can you change? Are you in control of your own destiny? These are but a few of the things for which we can all be grateful.

Thanks Changes Others

Here's a fun experiment. Take the time to tell someone today how much you honestly appreciate him or her. Now this does not have to be some soap opera moment with hot, romantic glances and swelling violins -- although you can do that if you like.

Simply take time to think about what the person you choose means to you. What impact do they have in your life? How do they make your world richer by simply being there for you? Once you have zeroed in on that, take a moment to tell them sincerely how you feel and thank them for their contribution. Now watch their eyes as you tell them.

Thanks Changes the World.

Once you take the time to sincerely thank that special person in your life, you will have changed the world for the better. Now that person will take those good feelings and probably pass them on to others.

Think of the impact you could have on the world if you simply took the time once a day to single out a special someone and show them sincere appreciation. What if that person caught the "Thanks virus" from you and passed it on to just one other. Now what would happen if only one person a day began to do this?

To think ... one simple attitude and one simple action ... changing you, changing me, changing the world. When you develop an "attitude of gratitude," you crowd destructive emotions from your heart and mind, become happier and make others happier too. I call that a win-win-win.

Letting the feelings associated with gratitude surface is one of the best ways to pivot from any negative emotions. Think of the people who make you smile and the people who you are blessed to have in your life. Then, think about the work you thoroughly enjoy. Finally, think about how great it is that you are able to sit in comfort and read this book. Wow! I bet I made you smile. See, it wasn't difficult and it works rather quickly!

Since reflection can turn a mood around, why not share the wealth? Instead of just taking pleasure from what has made life better, why not give some back? Call up those friends who are always there for you and let them know how much you appreciate them, or how about that teacher who inspired you to continue your education that helped you land the job of a lifetime, or your parents, children, or spouse who encourage, support, and motivate you. It is so easy to take the people who you always see for granted, simply because they are always there.

But what if they were not? Letting people know they play an important role in your life and they are valued is one of the most precious gifts that can be given. And it's free! It is funny how praise, gratitude, and appreciation work. When you take the time to be generous with others, you attract and therefore receive more.

Coach's Corner

Practice thanks.

Sometimes an attitude of gratitude takes some practice, especially if you've been experiencing rough times.

Thank your best friend for loving you. Thank your cat with a special can of tuna. Thank your chair for holding you comfortably. Thank the cashier at your local grocer for bagging your groceries. Thank the person standing in line ahead of you for her smile. Blow a kiss to that sweet man who let you into the lane during rush hour traffic. Thank the driver who didn't let you in for not hitting you. Just "thanks".

Pay It Forward and Create Miracles!

*S*peaking of being thankful, how about paying it forward? Most people would jump at the chance to help someone else, especially if it required very little inconvenience. There is a way you can make it happen -- by paying it forward. I know you may be asking, "What in the world is 'paying it forward?'" Many of you may have seen the movie, *Pay It Forward*. Paying it forward is the opposite of paying it back!

When someone does you a favor, what do you typically say? "Thanks so much (Sue, Charlie, or John), I'll pay you back!" Well, instead of paying back Sue, Charlie, or John, you do something nice for someone else. Awesome idea, huh! Only instead of paying it forward once, do it twice! Thus, one good deed could spawn hundreds of others in a relatively short time as you ask others to pay it forward instead of paying you back. Imagine the good that can be accomplished.

"At first, I thought that what I was supposed to give others was money, which I didn't have a good reserve of at the time. However, lately we have given many "things" of value away to the first taker. Odd how people expect that you'll expect something from them in return, when that wasn't the reason. I just did it because it felt right. The more I do it, the easier it is.

And what ended up happening was having twenty-some people show up to help us move when I was expecting four. I've gotten additional clients, had more fun, less worry, and a feeling of joy upon letting go."
~Mary

Trevor, the 12-year-old hero of the movie, *Pay It Forward,* thinks of quite an idea. He describes it to his mother and teacher this way: "You see, I do something real good for three people. And then when they ask how they can pay it back, I say they have to Pay It Forward. To three more people. Each. So 9 people get helped. Then those people have to do 27." He turned on the calculator, punched in a few numbers. "Then it sort of spreads out, see? To 81. Then 243. Then 729. Then 2,187. See how big it gets?"

The Pay It Forward concept of doing unselfish acts of kindness, a service for someone, and asking them to pay the kindness forward instead of paying it back is a powerful idea.

Tricia asked Mike to drive her to the airport to catch her flight. She did not want to leave her car at the terminal for four days. When she was almost ready to board, she told Mike that she would pay him back as soon as she got home. To her surprise, Mike told her she did not have to pay him back at all, but asked her to pay two other people forward. As she boarded the plane, she thought about his request and could not wait to try it out. She was so excited, by the time she returned home she had already fulfilled her end of the bargain.

On the two-hour flight, Tricia struck up a conversation with a fellow passenger and offered to help her break into a new market for her small business by introducing her to a few of her contacts. She exchanged business cards and sent the e-mails to her contacts as soon as she reached her hotel.

Her second good deed was completed when she offered someone a ride to their hotel when she learned the car rental had run out of vehicles. In essence, Tricia repaid her "debt" within hours of incurring it. And, by asking the two people she helped to also "pay it forward," she put the ball in motion for many others to benefit from this practice.

The best part for Tricia was the wonderful feelings that accompanied the acts of kindness. She was very happy she could help others, especially strangers, and that feeling carried over into the other parts of her trip. Tricia had a wonderfully successful trip, as like does attract like.

> *"When our light is shining bright, we have the*
> *opportunity to make a difference by fanning the*
> *flame of another who's light may be dim."*
> ~Eva

So remember the phrase, "why don't you pay it forward?" Be prepared to sit back and watch the rippling effect of how powerful and positive this is.

Coach's Corner

There are two ways you can practice "paying it forward". First, do a favor for someone today, and ask them to pay it forward to two people. Second, pay forward a favor someone else has done for you – pay it forward to at least two people, then enjoy the good feelings you'll have!

The Power of Letting Go

Now that you're feeling appreciative for all you have in your life, and have developed an attitude of gratitude, you may have come across a few persistent thoughts, beliefs, or feelings that tend to keep you down. Maybe you even got a little skepticism thrown your way when you tried paying it forward.

> *"Your thoughts determine your core beliefs.*
> *Your core beliefs determine the quality of your life.*
> *To change the quality of your life, begin changing*
> *your thoughts."*
> ~Eva

Still fuming at that ex-boyfriend who ran off with someone else? Do you cringe every time you think about going into work? Thinking you'll never forgive yourself for that decision you made fifteen years ago? You're not alone. It may be one thing to be thankful for all the good things in your life, and another entirely to let go of your past, especially the painful memories.

Carlos Castaneda said that one of the best things he ever did was to give up his past. This often requires a great deal of forgiveness – of ourselves and of others. It's hard to develop a positive attitude when what you're thinking about is all your failures, or how someone else has failed you. But, it's also important to let these things go if you really want to have more positive, magnetic thoughts. It's like trying to hike up a hill with a sack full of watermelons tied to your waist!

"I was determined to make my life work and the dominant thought was:

"I will find a way to make my life work. Life is meant to be good and fun. I will discover the secret of creation. I will learn how it is that life works. I will deliberately create events. I will attract the man that I want. I will be specific and I will give details to the Universe of my request."

I felt powerful! I married the man of my dreams. I became a mother after years of believing that I could not get pregnant, and all of these events have a story that demonstrates the Law of Attraction at work.

It has become very simple. Feeling is the secret of creation! Feeling is vibration; vibration attracts events, people, situations, and places into our physical reality."
~Annabelle

How many times have you said or heard the phrase, "But I have a right to feel angry"? Of course you have a right to feel angry or bitter or resentful. You have a right to feel any way you choose to feel. But why would you choose to feel angry or resentful? What value is there in holding on to the anger well past the event that triggered the anger? The person with whom you're angry has probably long ago forgotten the entire incident, and here you are still raging at his betrayal, indifference, or whatever.

And what about self-directed anger? Who hasn't done something in the past they regret? As you've seen, dwelling on these things will only dig you deeper into a hole. Well, do you know the fastest way to get out of a hole you've dug for yourself?

> *"The ability to let go opens the door for what we now need to flow to us."*
> ~Eva

Stop digging! Throw the shovel out of the hole and start climbing out by choosing thoughts that make you feel good, not angry. You can never climb out of a hole while you're still digging! Make the decision you want to climb up and out, then start climbing, one hand and foot after the next. But, this means you have to let go of what's behind you.

Forgive yourself and forgive others. We're all here to learn and grow, and in the process we all make some mistakes. We can't help it. Didn't you stumble a few times when you were first learning to walk? Are you still angry with yourself about that? Of course not!

Let it go! When you forgive, you naturally lighten up. Those watermelons are no longer tied to your waist. They're left behind and you're free to move ahead much more easily. And the best part of this is the other person doesn't even have to be in the picture! It's all within you – the choice to have a positive attitude and to let go of those nasties from the past!

Coach's Corner

Practice letting go.

Think of something you've done for which you're having a hard time forgiving yourself. Write it at the top of a page in your journal, then draw a vertical line down the middle of the paper, dividing it in two.

On one side write all the ways not forgiving yourself is keeping you from getting what you want today. On the other side, write all the things you'd be doing now if you forgave yourself. Pick a side you want to focus on and draw a big, fat "X" through the other side. Which side did you choose? Now, assuming you chose the side of forgiveness, take one action right now from your list.

Your Positive Attitude A-Z Feel Good Guide

*T*he Laws of Attraction are based upon being able to visualize and feel what you want to materialize in your life.

"One way that I started to feel good was to let go and let the Universe take care of things. Daily I wrote forgiveness letters, order forms to the Universe, and a list of jobs for the Universe to take care of.

Then, every hour I asked myself "how am I feeling?". I would ramp up the energy by reading my plan for what I wanted to create and visualizing success. I stayed inspired by asking myself "is this a path with heart?" and "does this feel good?" If it did not, I didn't do it. It was that simple!"

~Sarah

Training yourself to think positively and reach within are awesome tools, but sometimes it can be nice to have a handy reminder! A good friend of mine has assembled a selection of thoughts to reach for, whenever you might need them:

• Appreciate everyone who shows up on your path.

• Believe in yourself at all times.

• Create your vision.

- Declare what you want and go after it with all your might.

- Experience every moment and observe those that are pleasant.

- Flow with the current; it's a lot more fun than paddling up river.

- Go, start, begin -- just do it, moving onward and upward.

- Help your neighbor and teach others how to fish.

- Inspire children by being the example -- life by demonstration.

- Just be in the moment, accept, allow, forgive and be grateful.

- Keep your faith, trust and know all is always well.

- Listen to the voice within, your inner coach -- you're full of wisdom.

- Make every moment magical by just being who you are.

- Namaste, which means "we are all one, pure and divine".

- Open up to oneness, the essence of joy.

- Polarity exists in everything. It's diversity that adds spice to life.

- Quit whining. Quiet your mind and have a real heart-to-heart with yourself.

- Reach for the thought that always feels better. It's out there.

- Serve others unselfishly and you serve yourself. Givers do gain.

- Teach others, learn from others. Share, share, share and grow!

- Utilize your powers of observation.

- Value the uniqueness of 'you' and share the 'you' with others.

- Will-power is within you to create anything you want to be, have or do.

- X-ray yourself through visualizations and see all the possibilities that exist.

- Yield to the child in you. Play, laugh, giggle a lot and have fun.

- Zap some zeal and zest in your life -- amp up your positive energy!

-- Dory Willer, The Inner Connection Coach,
www.BeaconQuestCoaching.com

Isn't this a wonderful guide? These are clear, concise, powerful, thought-provoking nuggets designed to remind you to remove doubt from your life and allow the things you

most desire to be attracted. Please feel free to use the A - Z Guide, and all of its truth, as a tool to keep you on your chosen path and help you reach your goals. Just wait and see how easy it will be to become an attraction-magnet in your life!

Now that you're doing a fabulous job of cultivating a positive attitude, how about doing some things that will really get your attraction muscles loose and strong? In the next section, I'll give you some ideas that will get old stuff cleared out of the way so you'll have lots and lots of room for all the goodies you'll be manifesting in the coming months!

Coach's Corner

Pick a letter, any letter.

Think of a letter from A to Z. Got it?

Go to the list on the previous pages, read what it says for that letter, and take the first action that comes to mind when you read what it says. Go do it – now. Yes, right now.

CHAPTER 4

Setting the Laws in Motion

"Letting go, cleaning up and clearing out your space -mental space, emotional space and physical space- literally allows the Universe to flow more abundance to you. Now is a good time to make room for the newer, better things that are ready to come to you." -- Eva

Clearing Out the Old to Make Room for the New

As most people begin embracing the Laws of Attraction, they'll soon hit several stumbling blocks. They may have some great movement at first, but soon enough "real life" sets in, and the old patterns reemerge. Some new disappointment comes along, and it feels so much like that same disappointment last year that they immediately think, "oh, yes, here it goes again." Then, down they spiral into the old stuff. Sound familiar?

Have you heard yourself saying or thinking, "Well, it works for her because... (fill in the blank)"? Or, how about this one: "every time I take a step forward, something bad seems to happen."

> *"As in all things, success is built*
> *from the inside out."*
> ~Eva

Are you ready to really embrace the Laws of Attraction with a vengeance? Are you ready to set your intentions and put these Universal Laws to use the rest of this year, and on into the next? If so, you'll want to do a little house cleaning to clear out the old beliefs and patterns so newer, higher vibrating beliefs can take their place.

Think of it this way. Say you want to buy some new clothes because the old ones don't fit right anymore (because you look so much better!). But, your closet is still full of the old clothes. Where will you put the new clothes?

Here's another example, one you may have heard. A

learned professor wanted to study Zen Buddhism, and traveled far and wide seeking great Zen masters. He soon became very full of knowledge, but held little, if any real understanding. As he sat across from one Master, he spoke of all the knowledge he'd gained through his research. The Master was pouring the scholar a cup of tea. He kept pouring and pouring until the cup was filled and running over with hot tea. The scholar stopped talking long enough to say, "What are you doing? The cup is already full!".

The Zen Master smiled and said, "This cup is like you. It is already too full to accept anything else. Until you empty yourself of all this knowledge, I cannot give you any wisdom."

The Laws of Attraction are like that. If your thoughts are so full of disbelief, fear, frustration, and memories of things that didn't work, there's no room for anything new – the things you most want to attract! This also applies to many other things in your life as well, including your living space, car, friendships, and health. What isn't working or is in disrepair? Are all your relationships up-to-date and without old issues hanging around?

Here is an exercise I use with my clients at the end of each year to get them ready for the possibilities of the year to come. It can be a lengthy process; in fact, I encourage you to spend as much time on this exercise as you need, be it twenty minutes or a few hours. You will not be disappointed. You can use this process at any time (now would be a good time!) and not just as an end-of-year practice. If you're just starting out with the Laws of Attraction, this process will really kick-start everything for you by making sure you're headed in the right direction, and with enough space available for all the goodness that will come to you.

*"The biggest obstacle that I cleared out that made a
great difference, was no longer thinking that there
is "something" or "someone" that has the final say
in my life.*

*Knowing that I have creative control allows me to
relax and not become so attached to specific out-
comes. My work is to get my feelings to match my
desires and be totally present with those feelings."*
~Annabelle

As you start this process, you may want some tools available to help you jog your memory about your past year.
Here are some things you may want to have handy:

- Your calendar
- Your journal
- Any notes from your coaching sessions if you
  work with a coach
- Financial records
- A friend or two to help you remember!

Also, as you do this exercise, it may be helpful to have several sheets of paper, where each sheet represents one area
of your life, including: friends, health, personal growth,
spirituality, money, career, home, possessions, fun, recre-
ation, etc.

The process consists of answering the following questions
with as much detail as possible. Remember, you'll be using
this information to "empty your closet" of old stuff so you
can make room for the new. So, don't dwell on anything,
and definitely don't find any more reasons to judge yourself harshly!

1.   Make a list of all your disappointments, failures, losses, upsets and breakdowns that have happened in the past year. Acknowledge what these items are simply by listing them. You're listing the items with the intention of making a decision about what you want to do with them. You can choose to let them go, carry them forward, or convert them into something new and different. Also list any judgments or bad feelings you're holding about yourself or anyone else, including decisions you did or did not make that you presently regret.

Identify the ones you are willing to let go and on a piece of paper, create a symbol that represents this list. State to yourself, "I now release all old energy back to the Universe and make way for all new possibilities coming my way. And so it is." Take your paper symbol and release the energy back into the Universe by burning it, burying it, or tearing it into tiny bits and throwing it away. This physical gesture does create a great release of energy.

Because the Universe wants to fill this new empty space with something, it is important that you complete this exercise, and also the exercises in the three subsequent chapters in this section. When you have a clear vision and specific goals, the Universe then knows exactly what to replace these negative things with.

Identify the ones around which you commit to making a new promise and hold onto them to include in your wish list and goals – your new intentions.

2.   Make a list of any unfinished business that is still occupying your thoughts or energy in any way. This would include any of your relationships, anything having to do with your health, your home, computer, car, office, files, clothing, and so forth. When's the last time you had your

teeth cleaned? Have you backed up your computer lately? Do you fret every time you're in the middle of a big, important document? List all these things as you did with the first list.

Identify what you want to do with each item on the list. Do you want to complete it? Delegate it to someone else? Simply let go and move on? What specific actions do you want to take to resolve anything that's taking your valuable energy?

3.   Make a list of all of your wins, successes, joys, delights, breakthroughs, and just awesome things that have happened to you in the past year. This is a chance to celebrate and own what you have become. Where did you step into your power and greatness? Please don't gloss over these. The little stuff does count and no modesty is allowed! It's time to validate and take ownership of all you have accomplished in your life up until now.

These are things you will not let go! They are what you will build from because they hold the positive feelings and foundation for your positive attitude. Allow yourself to smile when you think of all you've accomplished!

4.   What have you learned about yourself and your life? What insights have you gained? True insights have the transformational   capability to shift us into a new, more alive place. As we are blessed with insights, it is important to nurture and deepen these new understandings. These are our wonderful foundation for personal growth.

5.   What are you grateful for? This list might include some of the above, and/or anything else you truly appreciate about yourself, the people, the things or activities that are in your life. **There is a basic principle that whatever you**

appreciate and give thanks for will increase in your life.
Read that last sentence over because it is important. Give
thanks for that quarter in your pocket and it will multiply.
Feel sorry you only have a quarter in your pocket and sor-
row will multiply.

6.   What would be a fun, special, personal thing to do for
yourself in celebration of your accomplishments? How will
you honor yourself? You deserve it!

This is a powerful exercise designed to put your life in perspective as you prepare yourself to move forward with
power, grace, and ease. It sets the stage for your continued
use of the Laws of Attraction on a daily basis with your
loose ends firmly tied up. I guarantee you will rediscover
some wins you forgot about, learn some things about yourself, and you may even be able to eliminate some energy
drains and leave them in the dust as you move forward
into your new life!

Life is always full of possibilities and potential just waiting
for you. Luck is preparation meeting opportunity, and
there is an abundance of opportunity at all times. All you
have to do is clean the dust from your lenses so you can see
it!

Coach's Corner

Guess what?

I want you to actually do the exercise in this section, not just read about it. It is a very powerful exercise, and combined with the next three sections will greatly accelerate your ability to attract more of what you want.

Kick Start Your Attractiveness – Set Your Theme For The Next Year

*Y*ou've now completed a bit of housecleaning, right? The next major step is to start identifying what you want to come in during the next year to fill the now empty spaces. Do you know how a good book or movie just draws you in from the start? You get a sense that something very interesting is going to happen, and you sit mesmerized by the cascading images. You can't wait to find out what happens because the characters and story are so compelling that you become emotionally involved in what happens with them. Why not set up the story of your life over the next year in this way?

You can give a big kick-start to your attractiveness by setting a theme for how you want your life story to unfold over the next year. I'm not asking what your goals are with accomplishments by dates, or what your resolutions are going to be. Rather, what your vision or dream for the upcoming year is going to be. What do you feel energy or excitement around? What is it you will be able to wrap yourself around and embrace? What is the thing with which you can really connect? What engages your imagination and feels compelling - that "something" that makes you want to work towards it, give it life, and make it dance!

"The Laws of Attraction gave me permission to
follow my internal beliefs ... I always trusted the
Laws, but only practiced the Laws SOMETIMES!
I was on a mission to use them for everything ...
so I became consistent."
~Jeanna

I'm talking about a creative process in which you can use any tool or methodology at your disposal. Do you like lists? Write a list. Do you prefer to draw, or are you more auditory – hearing your vision rather than seeing it? This process can be as full of creativity as you desire. Some clients have created collages, others have picked a theme song and others have used menus as their theme.

Are you excited? Are you ready to create your theme? Ready to give it life and feel it pulse? This is your great movie, your thriller book that is being created. A block-buster on the way! Here are some questions to stimulate your thoughts:

1. If your vision were a piece of music, what piece would it be?

2. If your vision was from nature, what would it be? Perhaps it would be a tree, the ocean, a babbling brook.

3. What does your vision taste like?

4. What does your dream smell like?

5. Is your dream a color?

6. What other senses can you use to develop your vision?

7. What if your vision were a thousand times bigger? Describe what it would be.

8. Are you forcing anything? Where can you ease off?

9. What metaphor would you use to describe your

vision? (For example, a fragrant white rose, unfolding in the morning light.)

10. What can you take less seriously?

11. Are there any rules you are holding on to? What can you eliminate?

12. How would a six-year old describe your vision?

13. Ask yourself some "what if" questions. What if _____?

14. Add one outrageous or wacky element to your vision.

15. What part of your vision makes you smile and giggle the most?

16. Pretend you were describing this fabulous movie you just saw about your life in the next year. How does it end?

Use these questions as a springboard to jumpstart your theme creation. Be as free, wild and inspired as you'd like. It's your theme, something for you to create and watch it take shape and evolve over the coming months. This exercise is meant to be a fun and productive way to start your upcoming "Attraction Program".

"I think the defining moment for me was when my two-year-old nephew passed away. Up until he passed, my manifesting had been a mixture of visualization and force. I knew I could create but since I did not think I had ultimate control I had to manipulate, and could not allow myself to relax and enjoy the present.

*I was afraid that if I did not really control my
thoughts and did not do my creative visualization,
events would not happen the way I wanted. When
he died I even thought that I had not "prayed
enough" or visualized his well being enough. I was
devastated, not only because we lost him, but also
because I realized that I knew nothing about life or
how it worked.*

*I thought that all those books I read, workshops I
attended, and those hours praying and visualizing
was for nothing. Life made no sense and I felt again
powerless and full of despair. I knew something had
to shift, and that shift was to stop forcing, and start
relaxing more."*
~Annabelle

Once you've identified your theme for the year, take a
moment to think about who you are and who you wish to
become. See yourself one year from today.

1. If you could have anything you want and no possible
    way to fail, what would it be? What do you most want
    for yourself?

2. When you look back on this period of your life, what
    do you want to remember? What experiences do you
    want? What accomplishments?

Coach's Corner

Write a letter to yourself that describes where you will be one year from today based on the questions on the previous page. Date it and seal it in an envelope to be opened only by you, and put it in a place where you'll find it one year from today.

Enjoy it, and remember the sky is the limit!

Make Your Wishes a Reality

*D*id you enjoy the exercises in the previous section? Well, it gets better!

Each year, a couple of months before Christmas, there is a large retailer that distributes a Wish Book® for children. This book is chock full of all of the popular games, toys, gadgets, and gizmos a child could hope for. Wouldn't it be cool if there was one for adults? I bet the adult version of the Wish Book® would have items with a much heftier price tag, although some parents may find this statement hard to believe! Perhaps it would contain the picture of a larger home, a new vehicle, a powerboat, dream vacation, or a new business.

But alas! We come back to the financial aspect of our wishes. Most wishes require money, and this is often why many wishes are shelved. But there is a way to take those wishes off the shelf and make them a reality. In fact, you can start doing so today by changing the way you think about them, in essence, shifting your belief.

> *"It isn't what you have, but what you do with what*
> *you have that defines your success."*
> ~Eva

The key to shifting your belief is in the next sentence. *You are the master of your own destiny and the creator of your reality.* Yes, you are! If you find yourself questioning this, aha! You have uncovered the obstacle that has been keeping you from making your wishes come true.

"Even though many things were rough, what turned things around for me in practicing the Laws of Attraction was developing extreme gratitude for the abundance of the Universe, and the ease of letting go and letting God.

I always had the faith, but forgot how much I would need to forget! What has really shifted is that I don't have to do anything I don't want to, or do things in a way someone else believes is the right way.

I started becoming more aware of my thoughts and actions, and determining which fit my dream and which did not. Also, upon trying these actions, sometimes the dream shifted and was perfected. I laugh more, and am more at ease."
~Mary

Everything you want is within reach. You just have to believe. Start thinking about the things you've wanted that have materialized and determine what your thoughts were when they took place. I'll bet you just knew you were going to get that job, meet your mate, or find that house. What you believe really does actually occur. You have a team working towards your goals twenty-four hours a day, but if you are focusing on negativity or lack, unfortunately that is what will show up. Train yourself to really focus on your thoughts, the things that show up from those thoughts, and learn to shift your thoughts and beliefs when what you want is not materializing.

"Then, I lost my job and had no money. I had no choice, I had to trust the principles and believe they worked. I made a daily system for myself to use the

Laws and did so diligently for one month -
perhaps two hours a day.

I 100% trusted that this would work.
I had to trust."
~Sarah

By shifting your belief you can create your very own Wish Book®, your own personal catalog for wishes and dreams, full of wealth and abundance. You won't have to wait until the end of the year, or for a specific season. You can tap into it at will -- 365 days a year. Don't give up on your dreams when you could be just steps away from making them a reality!

Coach's Corner

Make a short list (maybe five items) that you know absolutely have to be in your Wish Book®. For each item, rate your belief in your ability to have this, on a scale from 1-10. That is, 100% belief is a 10, no belief at all is a 1.

If it is anything less than a 10, then there is something blocking your belief. To help unblock this belief, it helps to find evidence to support your belief in having your wish. Think about something related to this wish – finding the perfect apartment, meeting a wonderful person at exactly the right time – and dwell on this evidence for about a minute. See if your belief hasn't shifted a little. Keep doing this until you can feel your belief slide gracefully into that "10".

Goal Setting

C lose your eyes. Imagine that everything you desire is just a wish away. All you have to do is close your eyes, focus your thoughts and ask your genie to make your wishes, dreams, or goals come true. Wouldn't that be cool? What if you didn't have to rely on anyone else but yourself? Not even your own personal genie. Wouldn't that be even better?

> *"My greatest creativity comes when I can break out*
> *of having to know, and be willing to not know."*
> ~Eva

Think back to some of the goals you have had in your life thus far. How many of them did you really want to achieve, but for one reason or another never materialized? How different would your life have been if you had succeeded with the majority of them? As adults we've learned it takes time to achieve the things we want in life. But what if as children we learned how to increase the chance of goals being attained and the speed in which it happens. Wouldn't that be a worthwhile piece of education? The following is a tool the majority of adults have not heard of, practiced, or mastered.

The world's leading authority on personal and business success, Brian Tracy, writes his goals down every single day, not just one or two, but his six top goals.

How did he arrive at the number six? They represent the six major areas or resources of your life: body, brain, being, time, people, and money. But he goes further than just listing the goals on a 3 x 5 card. Brian Tracy affirms them as well. He writes the goal as if he already has achieved it, just like visualizing and speaking from the goal itself. To affirm your goal, begin it by stating that you are 'happy'.

Adding the word 'happy' helps one acknowledge they are in the current state of being. It is like a light bulb going on that helps you recognize the state of joy, and concentrating on the feeling will help you magnetize more of it. Couldn't everyone use a little more happiness and good things in life? The last step is to write down what service, product, or information you plan to render and in what quantity and quality: "I am happy to be providing excellent value by selling x number of products to x number of satisfied customers each day."

Why is this technique so successful? Because the 3 x 5 card is kept with you all day long, and read aloud a minimum of four times, at breakfast, lunch, dinner, and just before bedtime. The goals should be changed and upgraded regularly, but no less than monthly. This technique keeps your goals in the forefront of your mind, so you begin to not just want them, but to actually live them. The trick is to always think positively. Always think of what you want to achieve and not what you want to change, or the fear you may have associated with the goal (like failure).

Are you excited? Isn't this technique inspiring? If you are a parent, why not get into the habit of doing this yourself and introduce it to your children as early as possible. Imagine how much they can accomplish in life by using these wonderful tools, and the confidence that will result.

"People with high self-esteem seem to attract the best in life."
~Eva

Mastering the art of goal setting is just another step in climbing that mountain to success so why not start right now. And, as you'll see in the next section, this is a daily practice. I'll give you a number of wonderful tools you can use daily to exercise your Attraction Muscles. After all... you eat and drink daily, right? Why not practice attraction daily?

Coach's Corner

Get yourself a few 3x5 cards. Write the numbers 1 through 6 on each card, and choose one goal for each of the six areas of your life:

Body: Your physical goals
Brain: Your intellectual goals
Being: Your spiritual goals
Time: Your organizational goals
People: Your people goals
Money: Your money goals

Here's an example of how to write your goals: "I am so happy and grateful that I am full of physical energy and I'm in excellent health every day."

Then, write what service, product, or information you plan to render and in what quantity and quality.

Carry this card with you and read it at least four times every day for the next 30 days. Notice the choices you make, people you meet, and actions you take, and how those influence the attainment of your goals.

CHAPTER 5

Pearls for Daily Attraction

"There are pearls in every day with your name on them.
Set your intention to find them...deliberately live each
moment as if it were unique and special to you.
Count your blessings. Appreciate your magnificence
and the magnificence around you, and notice how
many pearls you uncover today." -- Eva

Be Inspired Not Tired

s you begin activating some of that positive energy you've been generating, you'll find yourself in the midst of a great number of inspirations. Pretty soon, however, it's easy to get overwhelmed by everything you feel you have to do. Before long, a lot of people who start down this path discover their motivation starts to fade. The original spark goes away, and it can feel like you're just going through the motions and you end up muttering "so what?".

Do you feel tired and drained more often than not? Are there things you know you have to get done, but you are lacking the motivation to do them? How about changing things around so they become "inspired" actions and not "required" actions?

> *"Inspired action is the difference between*
> *potential and actuality."*
> ~Eva

One definition of the word, inspire, is "to exert an animating, enlivening or exalted influence upon." Even the definition sounds like fun, does it not? I will go one step further and say it is also powerful and empowering. Can you imagine finding joy in everything, having life be lively and exciting on a regular basis? Inspired actions are those you get so excited about wild horses could not stop you from doing them, and they will usually flow effortlessly and quickly. Believe me, it is possible.

*In a period of darkness I became still, and lived in
the moment, no plans for the future. From this contrast of pain and hopelessness a desire for joy was
born. I wanted for me and my family to feel joy
again. I wanted something to happen that would
make us feel again the goodness of life. I decided that
I'd start focusing my desire on bringing a new child
into the family again.*

*It wasn't easy, especially after all the pain that had
happened with us. I wanted to give up on the idea
many times, but I concentrated on bringing up
within me the feeling of joy. Then, I got the news
that my sister-in-law was having a baby. I kept
bringing up this feeling of joy - while driving, in the
shower, before I went to bed, even though I was told
I couldn't get pregnant again.*

*A year to the day of my baby nephew making his
transition, I was pregnant!!!"*
~Annabelle

How does one become inspired and create a world of
inspired actions? It goes back to setting your intentions for
what you want, visualizing it, getting into the feeling place
"as if" it has happened exactly the way you want it, and let
the inspired action "come to you." Cool, huh? Sound easy?
It is.

But if you get stuck, you can work backwards by focusing
on what motivates you to complete your goal. Is it your
family, or having free time to play? Perhaps it is the satis-
faction of having everything checked off your "To Do" list.
Better yet, write down your tasks and your motivations.
Things seem to become more concrete, more "real" when

they are written down. These tools will help you turn a project or task into something that provides you with major inspiration.

Jack was in the process of writing what he termed his "great American novel." In fact, he had been in the process for four years and despite what he told his friends and family, he was not feeling very inspired. His novel had become the joke amongst his friends and the proverbial albatross around his neck. When Jack decided to set his intentions and visualize the outcome, he had a difficult time doing this. He realized he could not get into his feeling place because the story he was writing did not fuel his passion. He could not even visualize himself completing this book. His writing had taken a wrong turn, and instead of backing up or starting over, he had felt compelled to continue because of the expectations of others. Jack was so surprised and energized by this realization that he immediately started outlining the book he really wanted to write. Writing had become an inspired action and Jack did not feel like it was a required one.

> "Deliberately put your attention on thoughts and things that please you with the sole intent of feeling good, and everything else will fall into place. It is as if by magic and yet it is not. It is Universal Law at play and it works every time without exception."
> ~Eva

So, what are you waiting for? There is no time like the present. Find a quiet space, turn on your favorite music, light a candle, and get busy setting those intentions to create inspired actions. Remember, inspired actions will make you feel alive -- before: due to the planning and anticipation; during: as you will be relishing actually putting your desires to action; and after: when you are remembering the

task and your feelings while it was being done. So, get out your pen and paper and get busy. The time has come to be inspired, not tired!

Coach's Corner

Make one action on your "To Do" list an inspired action. Pick something on your list you know you want to do.

What's the vision this task will fulfill or move you toward? Don't have one? Then, create your vision, or change the task to fit your vision!

Feel yourself completing this task easily, effortlessly, and playfully. Really feel this happening. Feel yourself inspired by the ease at which you complete the task. Now, go ahead and take action!

Shhh... Relax and Be Still

Yes, inspired actions are good. However, what about the "action" of stillness? Do you ever feel like you're being thrown around by all the things to do, like a rubber duck in a massive storm? Sometimes when everything gets so frenetic and busy, it's really difficult to remember it's all just about feeling good. How can you possibly feel good with all this "stuff" that has to be done?

> *"In our constant strive to reach the next goal, we forget to value where we are. To value the plateau is to value the serenity of the Now."*
> ~Eva

Blaise Pascal, the French mathematician, once said, "Almost all of our woes come from not being capable of remaining in our rooms." Pascal referred to fostering an ability to be with ourselves. It feels as though being alone these days is something of a privilege, a prize to be won after a hard day at the office. I find some of my greatest insights and my moments of most profound peace in the still moments of solitude and silence. It's these quiet times that I see myself most clearly. I can feel my body, sense the deep desires that long to emerge and calm the incessant chatter of my mind. Sometimes I get only fleeting glimpses of the quiet between the noise, but in those moments, I can recognize and feel the joy that comes with stillness. It feels good!

Wouldn't it be great to remember on a daily basis what an incredibly powerful creator you are? Wow! Think of it! It's so easy to forget when we get embroiled in life's daily adventures. That's a really good time to stop, take a breath, go for a walk, get out into nature, and simply be still. Let your mind and body relax and remember it's all about feeling good! I try to remember the words of Sister Corita Kent, a Carmelite Nun who said:

> "And at some time in your life
> trying to be good
> may be to stop running
> and take time... to be quiet
> and discover who you are
> and where you've been..."

I'm not suggesting you buy a pillow and sit cross-legged for hours in an ashram. You can play with stillness through simple breathing, listening to a babbling brook or taking a walk alone down a quiet street. You can meditate, take a walk on the beach, write in your journal, or sit in a meadow and watch the wind blow through the trees. Sometimes it's simply finding time to stand back, like a painter, and survey the activities that fill your life, discovering where and how you want to apply the next strokes of your brush and paint.

> *"There are thousands of opportunities to create what you want in every day. Unless you consciously and deliberately choose to focus only on what you want - and not on what you do not want - you'll find yourself in negative situations, circumstances and emotions. Make your dominant intent in every moment to focus on what you want and on feeling good."*
> ~Eva

Stillness brings with it fresh insights, new ideas, and a sense of wonder at the simplest things. How often do some of your most profound ideas come just as you're falling asleep? Why not create that same moment of quiet in your waking life?

Coach's Corner

Find yourself a nice, quiet space, preferably outside in nature. Go ahead and take your journal with you. Plan on spending about 30 minutes in your spot, alone and with all normal distractions like cell phone, TV, other people gone.

Close your eyes and breathe deeply for about a minute. Just let your mind wander as you breathe. Then open your eyes and spend the next 29 minutes noticing. Notice the birds, sky, flowers, trees, animals, people, and anything else. Notice how it feels to be sitting. Notice your thoughts. When you're finished, make a note in your journal of any insights or inspirations you received.

Speak from Your Heart with Kindness

Each of us is graced with the most powerful gift. With it, we are able to make people soar out of orbit with happiness, or plummet to the earth with despair if we are careless. What is this almighty gift? It is the gift of words and the ability to communicate.

As a society we often forget how powerful our words can be. We are occasionally reckless or too quick to speak when we should take time to think about the consequences of our words. We are taught from childhood to think before we act, but sometimes neglect to think before we speak!

This can be a thing of the past by learning the art of "speaking with integrity." Integrity is defined as "the quality of possessing and steadfastly adhering to high moral principles or professional standards." Right away, it elevates the position of the speaker to a place where he or she is responsible for caring about how their communication is going to be received.

Want to try it out? For the next week, examine your communications and try to speak with integrity. If you slip, jot it down and write a response that does come from a place of integrity. With practice, you will start to put this to use naturally and you will see how extraordinary the results will be. Your life and the lives of those you touch will be so much richer.

Now that we've decided to change how our words affect others, what about how our words can affect us? As a whole, we so often use our words to speak against ourselves. We were all taught manners. Isn't it a shame we don't apply these same wonderful, loving, helpful manners on ourselves? In fact, I bet if anyone else spoke about us the way we do, we would not be speaking to them at all! Make a conscious effort to speak positively to yourself.

In the story portion of the book, *The One Minute Millionaire*, the main character was told to wear a rubber band around her wrist and to give it a tug every time she had a limiting thought. Within days she had a red welt on her wrist, but as time went on she was pulling the rubber band with less frequency. Why not try this tool yourself? I challenge you to put that rubber band on your wrist and give it a good pull each time you speak about yourself in any way other than an exemplary manner. You may start out with a very sore wrist, but you will end up with a very strong sense of self.

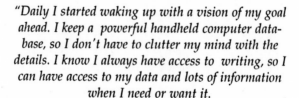

"Daily I started waking up with a vision of my goal ahead. I keep a powerful handheld computer database, so I don't have to clutter my mind with the details. I know I always have access to writing, so I can have access to my data and lots of information when I need or want it.

I did my best to avoid looking back at errors, so I could be starting fresh each day. And, I think it was this freshness that kept me in inspired action."
~Mary

We've decided not to speak to others without integrity, and to speak about ourselves in an exemplary manner. How about how we talk about others? It is gossip when we speak about others. It can be hurtful and sometimes have serious consequences, not just for others, but for ourselves as well. When we gossip we are tarnishing ourselves. Most of what is considered "good" gossip is negative in some manner. We are willingly corrupting our world by participating in such actions. Since we know that like attracts like, we are knowingly sending negativity out into the Universe. Make a promise to eliminate all forms of gossip from your life. Each time you think to gossip, instead turn it into a positive affirmation about the person. This change alone will help you attract much more of what you want.

Imagine how much good the "art of integrity" can put out into the Universe. Providing a positive, truthful comment, helping someone turn a bad mood into a good mood, and speaking to ourselves with only love will have an incredible affect on many lives. Remember the Laws of Attraction are at work at all times. Watch your words and speak only of what you would want to have in your world.

Coach's Corner

Practice the art of integrity. Find a rubber band that fits loosely around your wrist. Now, every time you catch yourself saying something negative about yourself or anyone else, give the rubber band a little pull so that it snaps back against your wrist. The secret to this technique working is to snap it hard enough so that it hurts (please don't draw blood!). Notice how much more infrequently you say negative things!

What Did You Just Say?

*S*peaking of integrity and the power of your words, we all know the classic amusing explanation of why you should not assume, because it makes an "A** of U and Me", but assumptions can be much more serious. An assumption can make way for hurt feelings, misconceptions, and resentments. When we make assumptions we completely de-emphasize another person's feelings for the sake of filling in the blanks that exist in our own minds.

Why do we make assumptions? Assumptions occur when we do not have a clear picture of what the other person is trying to say, or when we do not understand their actions. How can we eliminate the need to make assumptions? The answer is: by fully listening and asking questions. The average person does not fully listen when they are being spoken to. They are thinking of what they want to say next, what must be done, the task they were performing before the person interrupted them, or a multitude of other things. But the fact remains, they are not fully engaged in a conversation.

I'm going to use a classic cliché. The husband is watching a football game on television; his wife walks in and decides to hold a conversation with him. He "Yes Dear's" her, but in reality his attention is on the game and he has not heard a single word she has said. She realizes he is not paying her any attention and walks away upset. He was clearly not fully engaged in their conversation. He could have asked her nicely to speak with him after the game. He also could have taken his attention away from the game by turning it off for the duration of their conversation, or his wife could have waited to approach him until after the game. Any of

these solutions would have helped them avoid hurt feelings.

"My family is very important to me. Their well-being means my well being, and my desire for joy was stronger than the pain. My conscious decision to be happy again has always kept me going and my belief that the night may be dark and scary but joy comes in the morning has always sustained me. This is a basic assumption I make about life.

My assumption is that no matter how great the pain, joy can prevail if we so desire - joy is always present. I was born to be happy and damn it, I'm determined to do it!!!"
~Annabelle

Why are questions important? Questions allow us to eliminate the assumptions. But if we are not fully listening, we will not know the right questions to ask. Questions help clear up any miscommunication. With all of our differences, it is no wonder that what we mean and what we say may not be what someone else hears. A simple, "Do you mean...?" could help a great deal. Don't be afraid to ask questions. Questions let others know we really were paying attention while they were speaking. Everyone likes to feel as though they are being valued. One little question could make all the difference in someone's day.

4 Tips for a Fully Engaged Conversation
Free from Assumptions:

1. Just Listen

Don't think of possible responses or questions while the person is speaking. Don't interrupt. Never interrupt while they are speaking and don't try to solve the problem until they are finished detailing it.

2. Be Loving

Don't pass judgment. Listen with love and acceptance. An opinion or behavior that is different is what makes each of us unique.

3. Be Available

Be fully present with your whole heart, mind and spirit. If you cannot do this, wait until you can. You will both benefit.

4. Ask Questions

Once you have finished listening, ask questions to make sure you fully understand the situation. If you "think" you understand, ask questions until you "know" you do.

Coach's Corner

Take note of your conversations and see how well you fully listen. Make it a point to only listen when you can be fully engaged, and re-schedule conversations if you have to. Determine if you are asking enough questions to overcome the natural need within to make assumptions. Your conversations will have much more meaning to both participants. You will have all the information necessary to offer help or advice, and the person you are conversing with will feel they are important enough to you to have your full attention. It will be a mutually enlightened conversation.

Are You Be-ing?

The last few chapters have been a bit on the heavy side, asking you to pay attention to what you say and the assumptions you make. It's time for you to play a little more.

Remember when you were young and played "pretend"? You could be anything you wanted to be. There were no boundaries or obstacles. Do you recall the fun you had being free to imagine yourself as a fireman, doctor, ballerina, or professional athlete? It was fun wasn't it? If so, why did you stop? Perhaps because it was time to grow up and be responsible? How limiting. Now's the time to begin embracing your childhood again. (It's okay to say "yippee!")

As adults we often want something, but our belief that we can't achieve our desires end up standing in our way. It is time to suspend doubt and disbelief. The way to do this is by acting "as if"!

> "Whether you think you can or whether
> you think you can't, you're right."
> -- Henry Ford

Do not wait for the proof that you can be, do, or have what you want. BE it now in your mind. You can create whatever you want by choosing the be-ing appropriate to your situation, since we become what we think about. Look back on your life for evidence. You'll see that whatever showed up was a direct result of how you were be-ing. So, if you want different things to show up in your life, you'll want to change how you are be-ing! And, changing how you are be-ing means you'll have to change how you're thinking.

"Whenever your thoughts are on what you don't want, you are creating by default. You are creating deliberately when you are aware of your thoughts and consciously thinking of what you do want."
~Eva

Kelsey was beginning to lose hope of ever quitting her day job. She had been moonlighting in her home business as a virtual assistant for over three years, and still had not managed to come close to making what she was earning at her day job. In desperation Kelsey hired me as her personal coach. I had her develop an Ideal Client Analysis by assembling a list of all of the qualities she most wanted her clients to possess. By beginning with this exercise, Kelsey realized more than half of her clients were not her ideal clients. Some did not pay on time, others tried to monopolize her time, and she even had a couple that were not very nice. I then had her visualize what she thought her life would be like if she only worked with her ideal clients for the next month. Kelsey had visions of more free time, enjoying the work she was doing for her ideal clients and being paid what she felt her services were worth, in a timely manner. Kelsey was thrilled with the picture that unfolded in her mind. Kelsey was then asked to spend 15 minutes in the morning and 15 minutes at bedtime, visualizing herself as the person that attracted her ideal client.

After one month Kelsey had some amazing things to report. She had gained eight new clients that paid her double what she had been making, and she had started letting clients go that did not fit her ideal client analysis. Kelsey had learned she was allowing herself to be walked on, and by behaving differently, she would be able to quit her day job rather quickly. It all came down to her choosing what she wanted to think and how she wanted to behave in order for her to attain her goals.

One of the best things about games is the safety factor. Whatever shows up is fine when it is considered "Just a Game". Imagine being able to attract everything you want in life, just by deciding to be the one the lifestyle belongs to. How cool is that? Remember to keep it light and above all else, have fun with it!

Coach's Corner

What are you wanting that isn't now showing up? Imagine yourself having these things – they're here, and you're experiencing them fully. Who did you have to BE in order for these things to show up? Assertive? Focused? Determined? Passionate?

Decide who you have to be in order to have what you want, then find one way today to be that.

Be willing to let go of anything that does not feel good.
Be willing to reach for the thoughts that feel better.
Be willing to be embraced by your inner guides.
Be healthy, wealthy, happy, vital and alive.
Be in appreciation and gratitude for the overall well-being of your life.
Be in eager anticipation for what you are wanting to come to you easily and effortlessly.
Be ready, willing and able to allow into your life the goodness that life has to offer.
Be you fully!

Like any new adventure, the first few times you practice a new behavior it will feel awkward. That's okay. It's like riding a bike – eventually it will become second nature.

Follow the Leader

*D*id you have some fun with that last exercise? Sometimes, however, it might be difficult to know how to be something we have never personally experienced. We've been told for years the best way to learn something is by example. That is why we are taught by teachers, use computer tutorials, and follow examples and illustrations in books.

> *"Every day is a new beginning, a clean slate. You get to choose how you want it to be. You can choose to change the way things have been, or you can choose to let them stay the same. Today is your opportunity to make a difference in your present and in your future."*
> ~Eva

But what about day-to-day life? Are there people you can follow, that intuitively know exactly what your needs and wishes are, so you can copy their actions or solicit their advice? If I had to guess, I'd say not. So how does one go about finding someone to learn from? Go look in the mirror. You can achieve the things you desire most in life, by following your own lead. There is a three step process: **Being, Doing, and Having.**

How does one Be?

Personally I think this is the most fun part, because all you need is an active imagination and the strong desire to achieve your goal. This is when you focus your thoughts on your desired outcome, what your life will be like once you have it, who your friends are, where you are living, the job you may or may not have, the vacations you are taking, and so forth. This is when you get to live your desires, to plot them, to visualize them, to breathe life into them. The entire time you are exploring the "being" part, make sure you use all five of your senses: sight, hearing, taste, feel and smell. The use of your senses will make your goal that much more real. It will also provide you with powerful triggers when you encounter that smell or taste during the course of an ordinary day. Begin living your life as if you already are what you want to be.

> *"Fulfillment comes in living*
> *with direction and purpose.*
>
> *Consciously fill every day with*
> *positive purposeful direction."*
> ~Eva

The next step is Doing. Does this mean you will actually have to come up with a plan for how to reach your goal? Not at all! Have faith... it will come to you naturally. Once you experience the "being" stage, you will undoubtedly realize you feel compelled to pursue a course of action, make a call, greet a person, etc. Typically things you normally would not do, would hesitate to consider, or would outwardly scoff at are what you may be inspired to pursue. These are called inspired actions, as they result from you being in tune with your goals. The "doing state" will propel you even closer to your desired outcome. Let the action happen. Don't stand in its way.

The last step is Having. All too often people ask for things and when they are on the track to receiving them, perhaps just steps away from the finish line, things go awry. Why does this occur? Because they allowed themselves to make it through the first two steps, but stopped just short of attaining their goals. Silly, you say? Yes, but quite easy to do and very understandable. It is in this stage where nega-tive self-talk can interfere wildly. "Oh, come on, you're never really gonna get _____" or "Oh, puhleez, you can't _____" Does either of these statements or similar ones sound familiar? If so, perhaps you can recall a situation where you were THIS (holding fingers a millimeter apart) close and your _____ fell through. Well, silence those voices. Stop them now. Don't wait.

Coach's Corner

Sit down in a relaxing atmosphere and think about the things you want. Practice **"being"** in the lifestyle you want in your mind, and to bring it to life, write it down in your journal. Allow yourself to fully experience the joy that comes from achieving your dreams. Once you get a taste of this and nurture it, it will be easier for you to see your goals, and harder for you to convince yourself that you are not worthy. When you engage all your senses, you will be better able to recognize the nudges that will help you **"do"** what you need to do to succeed. You are entitled to have your goals come to fruition. Allow yourself to reach the top of your mountain ... to **"have"**. Get out of your own way. It's time ... follow your lead.

Are you Careful or Careless?

*A*s you are imagining your success, feeling, seeing, tasting and experiencing all the elements and attributes of the glorious manifestation of your dreams, you'll be using words to describe your inner experience. Many of these words will be words you use in your daily life. Are the words you're using in alignment with your internal image, that perfect little gem of a visualization you created?

The average adult typically utters 40,000 words each day, according to a study performed by Professor Robin Dunbar of Liverpool University. A substantial amount, but have you actually considered how valuable words are? What about how powerful they are? Words have the power to heal, lighten, comfort, and encourage. On the flip side they can wither, hurt, anger and discourage. What a gamut!

What about the role words play in life? The spoken word is a continuation of our thoughts. Do you always think carefully before you speak? Do you speak with good intentions? While it's quite normal to have negative thoughts from time to time, just because we think it, it does not mean it bears repeating. Thinking something and giving it a voice just solidifies the thought. So if it's negative, we've provided the nourishment for it to take root and sprout – just like a weed.

Ask yourself this question when you have a negative thought and are ready to utter the words: Do I want to see these words manifest in physical form today? Another question to ask yourself: Is what I'm about to say empowering or not? If it is not empowering, then how might you say it so it is empowering? If you can't, then it is best left unsaid! Do you want to attract negativity or lack? I'll wager the answer is no. If so, don't speak of it, about it, or repeat it. Easier said than done? Not really, but one must first become conscious of it when it is occurring.

"Music has always inspired me so I use music to keep me focused. When I wanted to attract a mate, I played "It's Raining Men" by the Weather Girls, or "Slow Hand" by the Pointer Sisters.

"When You Wish Upon A Star" is my theme song this year. I want to live my dreams always and always. When my nephew passed away, "My Heart Will Go On" was my song, as my way of telling him, I love you today and always even when I cannot see you. I want to know that you are here.

Music makes everything okay for me, as does writing, but it is easier to get inspired with music. Writing requires making the time, but it is also another way of keeping me focused and on track."
~Annabelle

Mrs. Morgan, a fifth grade teacher, was heartsick as she listened to the words that were being spoken by her students. They were very negative, often hurtful, callous words that had no business being spoken, least of all to other impressionable children. Having been on the receiving end of hurtful words during her school days, she knew personally how damaging the long-term effects could be. After a great deal of thought she formulated a plan. She discussed it with the school principal, and after she was given the okay, she sat down to compose a letter to the parents.

The following Monday, she assembled her class and explained her distress over the words that were spoken each day. She told them the principal and their parents were in agreement with her, and they wanted the behavior to cease. The students each had 200 minutes of free time each week that was used for recess and fun activities. She explained she was given permission to charge them five minutes for each instance of "careless speak" she heard. Like most children they did not take her seriously until about mid-week when the most serious offenders were removed from the classroom because they had no more free time available. By Thursday afternoon she had less than a quarter of her class for free time, and by Friday she had just one student remaining. The children that were removed were put to work in other classrooms or given additional lessons. The following week Mrs. Morgan saw a substantial improvement in behavior, and after doing this for three months the "careless speak" behavior was almost non-existent. The program was such a success that it was implemented grade by grade until the entire school participated.

Mrs. Morgan committed herself to making a difference. Are you ready to make a commitment? Make the commitment to yourself. The results will be phenomenal. You can begin to attract more positive things in life and improve your relationships. People who share your newfound control for voicing positive things will be attracted to you, and those who already know you will marvel at the new you. Your relationships will gather strength and new ones will abound.

As you firm up your commitment to using powerful, positive words, you will naturally want to share the abundance you receive with others. In the next chapter, you'll learn how you can actually accelerate the attraction of abundance in your life through the Law of Reciprocity.

Coach's Corner

Let the 40,000 words that you utter each day mean something. Remember to choose your words with care, speak positive words with conviction, and let attraction work its very powerful magic. Today, practice using words more powerfully. Ask yourself if what you are about to say is empowering. Catch yourself when you use "careless speak" and snap a rubber band on your wrist. Before the end of the day, you'll be speaking positively or you'll have a very sore wrist!

CHAPTER 6

The Law of Reciprocity

"There seems to be an innate quality in humans to want to serve others. Those who fulfill that need tend to lead the happiest lives." -- Eva

Reciprocity

*H*ow often do you think about the things you want? If you are like most people, the answer is very often. Teenage boys think about teenage girls once every three seconds. Is it any wonder we have to cajole them to get their homework done? Seriously, thinking about what you want too much might just lead to not getting it. Here's why.

In the Universe, there are principles. Gravity is a principle. Drop something and it will fall. One of the foundational principles of the Universe is called reciprocity. Although you may not call it by that name, you employ this principle every day. Let's take a closer look.

> *"The more I give, the more I have to give."*
> ~Eva

Reciprocity simply means the impulse we all feel to give something back when someone gives us something. This happens to you and me every day. Someone says "thank you", we say "you're welcome". Someone opens a door for us, so we open the next door for them. A waiter or waitress gives us outstanding service and we respond with a generous tip. Someone compliments us and we feel the need to return the compliment. We even use the phrase "return the favor," indicating a natural tendency to give back.

How does reciprocity affect your life? Here are two quick examples of how this foundational principle works in the real world. The more you understand and cooperate with reciprocity, the more successful you will become in every encounter you have.

Reciprocity at Home

You come home from a long day at work. You immediately begin to spill the beans about how rough your day was, how you are not being treated fairly, how life is tough. How do you think your spouse or children will respond? Chances are they will respond in kind by letting you in on their day and its disappointments. While these mutual pity parties aren't fatal, they don't set the stage for a great evening.

How much better if, when you tell your story, you find the good in your day. No pie in the sky. No denying that some things are tough. Just finding the silver lining and choosing to count your blessings instead. Now how will your family respond? The odds are they will follow your example. If so, you have set the stage for a wonderful evening and made a super valuable deposit in your memory bank.

"The transition of my nephew filled my heart with compassion. Before his death, I knew how to feel sorry for me and others (especially for me). Feeling sorry is not feeling compassion, but is a feeling of being powerless.

Compassion on the other hand allows me to feel the pain while knowing that well-being is always present and that goodness abounds. My dominant desire for me and others is joy, joy, joy, and always joy. And by vibrating to this dominant thought life has responded. It feels better than pain.

That's the simple truth."
~Annabelle

Reciprocity at Work

Reciprocity is best expressed in our work environment by giving great customer service. We all have a choice when it comes to serving customers. Will we do what we have to do and call it a day ... or will we go the extra mile and provide a WOW experience for our clients or customers?

When we choose to go the extra mile, giving of ourselves, we are rewarded with repeat business and referrals. Thus, the principle of reciprocity kicks in and we receive after we give. What happens if we choose to just give average customer service? Not much.

Let me encourage you to think about the Law of Reciprocity in your life today. Maybe even discuss it with someone at lunch or dinner. The more you think about how you can give, the faster you will achieve your goals. In fact, you will find that it is universally true that when you give ... you will receive.

Coach's Corner

Are you ready to practice reciprocity? The easiest way is to give good words. Today, give only good words. Say something nice to a stranger. Compliment people you know. Say a good word to the grocery store clerk. Speak nicely to your dog. Go throughout the day saying nothing but good words, then see what comes back to you.

Tithing - By Giving You Will Receive

*D*id you know that water, when it is simultaneously frozen and exposed to a photograph of a chamomile flower, will create crystals in the shape of that flower? Dr. Masuru Emoto, physicist and author of Messages from Water and More Messages from Water, has demonstrated that thought has a direct effect on water. Thoughts of love and prosperity will create exquisitely beautiful water crystals, while thoughts of anger and hate will cause the creation of misshapen crystals.

> *"When you appreciate, your Source Energy flows through you. When you are blaming, your Source Energy is shut down. Make a conscious effort in every day to flow your Source Energy... by appreciating, by praising, by basking, by loving."*
> ~ Eva

What's this got to do with tithing? First, our bodies are mostly made of water. What you think about directly affects every cell of your body. Second, Dr. Emoto's experiments show that nature itself is both holographic and interconnected. What you think about, and the actions you take, even at the minutest level, creates perhaps billions of replicas of those thoughts throughout the Universe. Mind boggling, isn't it?

Tithing can be one of the purest actions of prosperity. To give is to say to the Universe, "there is abundance". The essence of abundant thinking is that all can prosper, and by giving, you open the door to receiving, and by receiving you can give even more.

Why is tithing something so many already successful peo-
ple believe in? Perhaps, because they recognize the cycle of
the Universe that says in order to make room for more, we
have to let go of some of what we have. It's a classic win-
win for everyone involved. Many children practice this.
Here's an example. Sue and Jane are playing. They both
come inside for a drink. Jane runs outside, trips and spills
her fruit punch. Sue takes the remainder of her punch and
pours it into her friends' cup. Her mom sees this act of
kindness and brings her a full glass of punch. Sue has just
been rewarded for her selflessness and in fact received
more than she gave. Tithing is based on the same principle,
substituting money for fruit punch of course.

*"I do generally like to be of contribution. It provides
a lot more balance in my life and it feels right."*
~Jeanna

A common convention is to tithe, or give away 10% of one's
income. I know the idea of giving away 10% of all income
has your eyebrows raised, especially if you are presently
not in a very good financial place. But I assure you good
will come of it. First, you get to decide where you would
like your gift to go. Is there a shelter in your community or
a youth center that needs assistance? Or perhaps your son
or daughter's school is in need of supplies? It's your gift
and you have control over deciding where it would be of
the most benefit. This alone can make you feel good inside.
And those good feelings will create millions or billions of
happy water crystals. Guess how strong the magnetic pull
of a billion happy water crystals will be.

Being able to help those less fortunate is always powerful with the Universe. Firstly it shows you are grateful for what you have and willing to help those less fortunate than yourself. Secondly, think of how beneficial your gift will be. Those on the receiving end will be giving thanks for the gift you gave, and putting their gratitude out into the Universe as well. It creates a huge chain-reaction of prosperity thinking, and it will all come back to you ten-fold.

Coach's Corner

Give it a try. Make a commitment to begin giving 10% of your income away to a cause that is close to your heart. Or begin just giving a little, even if it is less than 10%. Once you start, keep a journal and write down the new financial opportunities that begin showing up. Some of the things that others have seen manifest are: new job offers for a larger salary, new clients, new business ideas, partnerships or contacts that have resulted in more funds, and unexpected payments.

Practice Gratitude

*T*here is a form of giving that is pure and simple. It is the giving of gratitude. Thornton Wilder wrote "we can only be said to be alive in those moments when our hearts are conscious of our treasures." We can feel thankful for a lot of little things every day, even in the middle of life's challenges. I'm not saying you should be thankful you broke your arm or lost your job. But look around you in that moment and see what's been there all the time or what's never left in spite of the difficulties. Maybe it's the old elm tree outside your window, your cat, best friend, partner or your health.

> *"Acknowledging the good things in your life each*
> *day opens the door for more."*
> ~Eva

There's always something to be grateful for. Julia was bemoaning her work situation, convinced there was nothing at all good in it. These bad feelings permeated the rest of her life as well, so the whole picture looked rather bleak. When she decided to hire me as her coach, she brought her negative feelings up first thing, saying, "It's a complete mess, and there's nothing I can do about it". She wasn't in a mood to be grateful! I asked her to look at it from a different perspective. Julia was asked to look at her situation from the perspective of what she wanted, rather than what was awful. This was hard for her because she was so used to complaining about everything at work.

When Julia thought about what she wanted, she almost immediately noticed some of the things she already had – a nice house, good friends, and cuddly cat. She liked where she lived and liked that she was in pretty good health. Sure,

her job was still awful, but this new perspective of appreciation and gratitude for what she already had, helped her to slowly shift her energy. The remarkable thing is that soon after Julia started shifting her outlook to one of gratitude, she was offered a job in a different department, and her job actually became fun again.

> *"Appreciation is the same vibration as love. Look for more things to appreciate every day and feel your connection to Source."*
> ~Eva

Gratitude, like trust and faith, is a muscle. The more you use it, the stronger it grows, and the more power you have to use it on your behalf. As you practice gratefulness your capacity to draw on its gifts will be increased. To be grateful is to find blessings in everything. This is the most powerful attitude to adopt, for there are blessings in everything.

There are times when gratitude is more difficult to come by. In the next chapter, I'll help you move through the difficult times of your life with more grace, more gratitude, and with a lighter spirit.

Coach's Corner

If you've already got a list of desires, pull it out. If not, now is a good time to create one.

Get out your journal and list everything you want. As you do so, look around and also jot down everything you already have. Once you've completed your list, take a moment and allow yourself to feel grateful for what's already here.

CHAPTER 7

When Things Don't Work (And You Want Them To)

"Regardless of your circumstances, make the best of
everything in your mind. As you do, you attract more
of the best to you." -- Eva

Is the Energizer Bunny Mocking You?

*A*re you missing your spark? The thing that makes you want to get up in the morning and sing? Why is that? What is it that's getting in the way?

The answer is probably that you have energy drains. One of the definitions of drain is to "exhaust physically or emotionally". Does this sound like what you are feeling? Do you lack the energy, drive, or ambition you would like to have in one or more areas of your life? If so, it's time to plug the leaks in your energy.

> *"In the pain of one door closing behind you, there is even greater opportunity in the door that is opening before you."*
> ~Eva

How do you identify energy drains? They are the things that leave you feeling unfulfilled, depressed, discouraged, exhausted, hopeless, or passionless. They can occur as a result of employment woes, too many demands, educational pursuits, relationships, health issues, or any other thing or person that touches your life. A very important point to remember is that energy drains are incredibly personal and unique, and have as much to do with your personal perspective as anything else. Something that is a serious drain to one person could be the ultimate passion of another. Take Helen and Naomi as prime examples of this point.

Helen is a working mom. She gets up at six in the morning, gets herself dressed, and carries her sleeping son into her babysitter's home by seven so she can begin her forty-five minute commute to work each morning. She thinks about Kyle often throughout the day and sometimes has to fight tears as she envisions the things the babysitter gets to see him do that she ends up missing. She had hoped by now she would be used to being a career mom, but she isn't. She can hardly believe she's been doing this for two years.

Naomi is a stay-at-home mom. She left a very lucrative career to stay at home with her daughter. It's been nine months and she is miserable. Katie is so demanding that Naomi barely manages to get dressed most days and never seems to be able to get anything accomplished around the house until after Katie goes to bed at night. Naomi feels isolated because she was used to the hustle and bustle of her office, but she shies away from spending time with other stay-at-home moms because they seem to enjoy the life she loathes.

> *"We have been trained to justify our worth through our struggle. And yet it isn't possible to justify our worth through our struggle, because in our struggle we aren't connected to our Source. And when we aren't connected to Source, we have nothing to give. It is in our feeling of joy and well-being that we contribute to the whole. Then, we are contributing in significant proportion."*
> ~Eva

It seems as though Helen and Naomi would each find their passion and eliminate their drains if they could switch places. Short of this ideal situation, let's see what other things they could do to alleviate their drains.

Helen is unhappy because she spends so much time away from her son. If Helen had to keep a full-time job, she could be home for most of her son's waking hours if she found a second shift job working 3:00 until 11:00. If she could make do on a part-time wage, her flexibility would be even greater and perhaps she could work solely during bedtime hours.

If Naomi felt strongly about being home with her daughter, she could start a home-based business and have someone on hand to provide childcare if it were the type of business that did not allow for distractions. She could also contact her previous employer to see if there is any way she could still remain involved with the company in a home-based capacity. This way, she does not have to develop new business relationships and will be able to be on hand for her daughter.

In order to change the things that were draining them, these women had to determine the problem, be willing to say no to the things that were draining them, and decide what solution they wanted to say yes to in its place.

Unfortunately, there are times when we are unwilling or unable to say no. So, what then? That's when you need to decide how to change your perspective so you are okay with things the way they are.

> *"The Universe/ God tossed a chronic disease at me, and sometimes I let it get me down. Worse, I let it get others down. By knowing that even this is just another challenge that wouldn't have been sent my way if I couldn't handle it, I persevered. What is interesting is that answers, cures, and natural remedies came out of the woodwork! I don't dwell on the negative anymore. I just pick up and move on. Sometimes I'll chant a mantra that works for me, like simply saying "Next". This helps me move on."*
> ~Mary

Let's say you decided you wanted to eat healthier and exercise for weight loss. But each time you put yourself on a regimen, your plan completely fell apart, leaving you feeling drained. This might be an ideal situation to determine you are okay with not doing the healthier eating and weight loss program at this time -- perhaps shelving the plan until a later date, or reducing the number of days that you plan on exercising. There are many situations like this in life. Don't let them drain you needlessly.

Ultimately, you are the captain of your ship. Only you can determine exactly what you can and cannot tolerate. Have you identified your drains? Once you do, you must put plans into action to make your energy drains go down the drain! Be willing to say no to the things or circumstances or people that drain you and replace them with what you do want. Get rid of your drains today and recharge your batteries for a passion-filled existence.

Coach's Corner

Get your journal out and make a list of everything you're tolerating, or that is somehow draining your energy. On one side of the paper, write what is draining you, and on the other, write how you'll feel when this is resolved.

Put yourself in the feeling place of how it will be, then quickly jot down any ideas that come to you to resolve those energy drains once and for all. Your best resolution comes from these positive feelings and not from feeling badly about the situation.

What If "No" Isn't An Option?

Sometimes saying no isn't an option to certain energy drains, maybe at work, in a relationship, or in other areas of your life. Like Helen and Naomi in the previous section, you might not have any other options that immediately present themselves. It might be Naomi can't afford any help, and it would cost her more to go to work than stay at home. Helen's job may be the only thing keeping her family clothed and with food on the table, and working part time just isn't an option.

What then? I had mentioned changing your perspective to being okay with the way things are. First, I want to remind you that you always have a choice. At any time, any place, you can choose to be where you are, doing what you're doing. If Helen and Naomi really believe they have no other options, then what would happen if each actually chose to make the best of their situation?

> *"No matter what situation in which you find yourself, you always have a choice. Always! Tap into your inner wisdom and deliberately choose your response from a higher consciousness, rather than reacting unconsciously."*
> ~Eva

Helen might actually look forward to the time she'll spend each evening with Kyle, and then choose to enjoy her 45-minute drive and play a little more at work. By changing her attitude and choosing to feel good about what she's doing all day, she'll naturally start attracting other things that will make her feel good. When she spends her time looking forward to seeing Kyle instead of feeling depressed that she can't see him during the day, she'll be more attractive to ideas, options, and people who can help her spend even more time with him. Options might suddenly appear out of nowhere, such as a job-sharing opportunity, or even a day care center opening close to her work. These will come naturally as a result of the shift in her attitude, and not because of anything she's doing directly.

The same is true of Naomi. What if Naomi realized how wonderfully fortunate she is, and chose to enjoy every single moment with her child? This positive energy would attract like positive energy, bringing in options she'd never dreamed of. She could be going for a walk in the park and meet another mother who's in exactly the same situation. They might make arrangements to give each other a short break every day.

The key thing to remember is that the Law of Attraction states "like attracts like". Regardless of your situation, when you choose to make the best of it, and decide to enjoy the ride while you're on it, you'll naturally become more attractive to other joyful thoughts and opportunities.

Coach's Corner

What's something you have to do today? Try choosing to make the best of it, and set the intention that it will be easy, fun, and effortless. Then, go ahead and do it with a lightness and ease.

Learn How to Make Fear Your Ally

*S*ure, you're choosing to go into that dead-end job because it seems there is nothing visible on the horizon. Could it possibly be that you have some fear of the unknown? Or perhaps you are completely aware of the things that make you fearful. Did you know that fear is the major cause of failure? It is not failure itself or the action taken to pursue an idea or dream, but the inaction that is the result of fear. Fear causes you to not take action, and at the same time puts you in a vibration that will attract more things of which to be fearful.

It is human nature to try to control the various aspects of life, yet fear is often allowed to wrest the control away. Why give anything that kind of power over your life? Isn't it time to stop letting fear hinder you from doing, being, or achieving what you desire? When fear is holding you back from what you really want, it is time to face it head on and move through it. How can fear be overcome? Actually it is not as difficult as it may initially look.

"I had a tendency not to trust in the outcome I desired. I would get attached and fearful that what I wanted wouldn't happen. Sometimes I'd get so frustrated that I FORGOT to use the Laws to make my life easy! I was thinking that I was allowing, but the result wouldn't show up that I wanted. I'd realize that I was still in doubt! Ah, the truth was painful!"

~Jeanna

Fear is a biochemical response to some outside stimuli. What you do with this normal biochemical response is entirely up to you! It's all in how you interpret the situation that causes either inspired action, no action, or a big retreat! Most of the fear that stops us from moving forward is complete fiction resulting from an incorrect interpretation of events. Please realize FEAR is nothing more than False Evidence Appearing Real! Knowing it is false is the key that shifts the power back to you and puts the ball back in your court.

The thing that moves you to take action, so you can face your fear, bring it to light and cause its power to dissipate is confidence and faith. Confidence is built up and the fear is transformed into excitement, which brings you that much closer to success.

There are five steps that can be taken to cross the barrier from fearful to fearless:

1. **Identify the fear or fears**. Make sure you are aware of the entire situation. It is not uncommon for more than one fear to be at the root of a problem, or a fear from long ago resurfacing to couple with a new one.

2. **Identify what is holding you back from being, doing, or having whatever it is that is desired.** You need a clear understanding of what must be overcome in order for you to successfully combat it.

3. **Identify what you would do if you didn't have that fear.** Visualize what your life would be like if this albatross did not exist. How would you feel? How many more opportunities would be available to you? How many more adventures would exist? How much happier would you be?

4. Identify situations when you faced fear and successfully moved beyond it. With a little thought everyone can identify situations where he or she moved beyond a fear to reach a desired outcome. A fear of change (a new relationship, a new job, graduation, a wedding, etc.) where you faced your dragon and triumphed! You get the gist! Use these times as "touchstones" you carry in your pocket to remind you that you can do this again.

5. Identify the qualities in you that helped you succeed. These are the qualities that are the foundation for your success and typically, the foundation for you as a person. Qualities such as tenacity, integrity, zeal, confidence, and being able to see the big picture, to name a few.

> *"When you take risks, there is the possibility*
> *of failing, and yet by not taking risks,*
> *failure is certain."*
> ~Eva

Spencer knew that it was time to strike out on his own. He had a business plan, had been putting away funds for his home-based business dream for years, and even had the support of his wife. But there was one thing holding him back -- fear! Spencer has always had an overwhelming fear of public speaking and knew that he had to overcome this fear if he was to make a success of his business idea. Spencer decided to try to put the five steps to work. He acknowledged the fear of public speaking, but realized he was most afraid of looking like a fool. Next, he came to grips with the fact his fear had cost him a lot. In addition to not starting his home-based business, his inaction caused the delay to be placed on starting a family.

He then thought about what his life would be like if these fears were not part of the picture. He would have had his own successful business, would probably be a parent, and most likely would have the home he and Sheila had been talking about for years. He knew public speaking was a surmountable fear because he had had success with several other fears over the years. When he identified the previous fears, he decided to call on the qualities that had helped him with those.

"Fear is always a pest, always trying to get my attention. Especially that "waiting for the other shoe to drop" feeling. I deal with it sometimes with impatience like a child that is misbehaving. Other times I reassure this gremlin that there is nothing to be afraid of and I talk to it.

Fear is not a monster under the bed, but is just a scared little child that does not want to get hurt. Some days fear does get to me and I just start all over. New day, new me, scratch all that and here I go again!"
~Annabelle

Determination, stubbornness, the desire to succeed, loyalty, honesty, and intellect had all come into play. He knew these were the basis for achieving victory.

When he looked at where he was, where he wanted to be and how he had attained success in the past, things began to click for Spencer. He knew he had to sign up for a public speaking class, had to make sure he felt knowledgeable about his subject matter, and had to start putting a plan together immediately so he could start applying his newly learned skills to his dream. He was driven to take the pause button off his life.

So, how are you letting your fears stop you? How can you take the pause button off your life? What are some of the qualities you have drawn upon in the past to overcome your fears and reach your dreams? Now is the time. Seize control of your life again.

Remember to focus on the end result - the success! Use visualization to get into the feeling place of how great it is, how successful you are, how easy it becomes and how joyful it is for you. Stop thinking of fear as your enemy, remembering that it is only False Evidence Appearing Real and embrace it as an ally!

Coach's Corner

This exercise is simple. Pick a fear you have that is a relatively small one. Don't pick your biggest fear to practice with! Then, go through the five steps in this section with this fear.

What actions come to mind as you go through these steps? What do you want to do next? How can you embrace this fear as an ally? What inspired actions come to mind? Write them in your journal and then take action!

Readying for the Harvest

*E*ven when you're diligently working through some of your biggest fears, you can sometimes get a nagging feeling that the Laws of Attraction aren't working in your life (and you'll definitely have those times!). Believe it or not this is the perfect time to get ready for the harvest.

When you think of harvest, do you envision arms piled high, full of good things? Well, in essence that is exactly what harvest is. It is defined as "the product or reward of exertion".

There was a very wealthy man who once said, "the most difficult thing of all was getting to the point where I fully realized how easy it is to make money". It seems that we're always struggling and working really hard to get what we want, but we spend very little time actually preparing ourselves to reap the rewards of all that hard work.

> *"The parts of ourselves we refuse to see have the greatest influence on who we become."*
> ~Eva

What do you want to harvest in your life? Do you need more time to get things accomplished? Do you need to de-clutter your home? Or perhaps, do you want to pursue some ideas to make more money? Since the word "exertion" is already present in the definition, I am sure it is no surprise that action is involved in the process. The key is to take action that comes only from inspiration!

So, how does one get ready for a winter harvest? First, over a period of one week, take several daily snapshots of your life. Second, use your snapshots as a tool for you to compose a list identifying the following three things:

1. What would you would like more of?
2. What no longer fuels your passion?
3. What have you allowed to persist that needs eliminating?

Try not to rush or force things as you are examining your snapshots. This is your time to determine where you are going to focus your energies to produce the most bountiful harvest of your life.

Did you determine you wanted more time in your day or more time for yourself? How are you going to create inspired actions for this task to become a full-fledged harvest?

"My greatest disappointment so far has been about money, which is of course related to my biggest fear. I have manifested more money easily and effortlessly! Yet, I have discovered that no matter how much I have in the bank I am always afraid that is not enough. I learned to handle this on a daily basis by listening to something that makes me feel at ease and uplifts me. I mainly do this on my way to work, and it could be an Abraham-Hicks tape or my favorite song blasting from the CD player. I take time to acknowledge my victories, like "tomorrow is payday and I am getting a big bonus check with my regular salary".

Life is a day-to-day assignment and the moment of power is in the present. The more time I spend being aware of the now, the less fear I experience.

*I can also experience many angry vibrations, which
keep me from being in alignment with my desires. I
can be so impatient and get frustrated quickly.
This is frustration built by focusing on what is
wrong. When I focus on what is right in my life,
the frustration dissipates."*
~Annabelle

Celia completed the previous exercise and determined she was short-changing herself big time! She was an awesome single mother, a dependable employee, and a great friend, but she never had any time to do the things that brought her joy and fulfillment. Celia decided she was going to create "me" time each and every day. She first determined how she spent her time each day and began by eliminating the things that were a non-productive use of time. Next, she decided to piggyback as many tasks as she could to increase productivity and to create larger blocks of time. Lastly, she decided to put a schedule, calendar, and list system in place so she knew all the things that were expected of her. This allowed her to plan approximately how much time would be spent on each task and note the actual times for future planning purposes. Celia had tremendous results. She was able to free up over two hours each day to spend on herself. For those necessary quiet moments, she gets up one hour earlier than her children.

"I have either total magic or total stalemate in my relationship (with lots of resistance) when I forget to expect what I want. One of the setbacks is not everyone believes or lives by the Laws so it takes some of the fun away when trying to support folks in creating their magic. Of course, I have lots of support and coaches who remind me to use the Laws. I've had lots of monetary success and also success with more play time."
~Jeanna

When Daniel completed the exercise, he determined he spent way too much time in a job that was completely passionless. He dreaded getting up in the morning and hated sitting at a desk all day. He knew he needed a purposeful job that was his passion and knew it was a monumental task that required both time and commitment.

Daniel decided he needed to break his task into small action steps. He decided to continue working at his job while he took six months worth of evening classes at the local craft store and a year's worth at the University. Daniel's passion was to become a home-based jewelry maker. He spent six months learning his craft, and then starting making jewelry in his free time during the last six months of business classes. Within a year, Daniel had a great inventory of products, had his own web site, and had even begun making sales. In eighteen months, Daniel felt confident enough to quit his job and has not looked back. He is now very happy that he followed his passion, and he watches his harvest grow each year.

"I see no point in looking back at what I didn't get done. I choose, instead, to acknowledge where I am and where I want to be; then I determine what steps it will take to get me there."
~Eva

Yvette knew her friendship with Adele was a huge mental drain for her. It was the essence of this relationship she wished to change for her harvest. Yvette wanted to let Adele know she valued her friendship, but she could not keep being her friend if Adele continued to spend all of their time together complaining about how negative her life was. Yvette listened to Adele complain week after week, and it seemed like Adele left their lunch feeling relieved and Yvette left feeling depressed. Yvette decided she was going to start putting the ball back in her friend's court. When their next lunch date arrived, as soon as Adele started complaining, Yvette asked her how she intended to solve the problem. This dumfounded Adele. It made her stop and ponder her situation. In fact, by the end of the lunch Adele had identified a number of goals that she wanted to pursue and was feeling energetic. Not only had Yvette changed this meeting for herself, but she helped her friend start emerging from a rut. Yvette was delighted that some creativity on her part salvaged her friendship.

Celia, Daniel and Yvette had all identified areas in their lives they wanted to work on for the harvest, and each took inspired actions to achieve their goals. What inspired actions are you going to take to ready yourself for the winter harvest? Whatever your list entails, remember the goal is about first taking stock and then taking action from inspiration to reap the plentiful rewards.

Your Best Is Always Good Enough

*R*egardless of how much effort many of us put into getting ready for the harvest, we have this nagging voice that somehow we haven't done enough. Do you remember that inner voice? You know -- the one we have to put a muzzle on and train? The one that says "we can do better," what we did was "not good enough," and even "you're a failure."

Can you tell why that voice needs to be silenced? First and foremost, because it is wrong! We gain nothing from beating ourselves up about things. In fact, it is a serious waste of energy that could be spent building ourselves up. By the way, remember we are only supposed to be speaking to ourselves in an exemplary manner, and if you're not, put that rubber band back on your wrist! (See the section, "Speak From Your Heart with Kindness" in Chapter Five).

Let's face it. We are human and we're not perfect. There are going to be times when you cannot give something one-hundred percent, just sixty, and that's okay as long as you're doing your best. Athletes and those who study them have shown that in order for them to perform at their peak level of performance, they have to have down time – time to rest and recharge. This down time is absolutely essential to their being able to have that 100%-plus focus during the critical times.

*"Be the best you can be by focusing on your
potential, not your limitations."*
~Eva

What is your best? Your best is whatever you are capable of in the moment. Will it change? Absolutely! I'll bet you are capable of performing better when you are feeling well, are well rested, and are fed, as opposed to sick, exhausted, and starving. Many factors can come into play to change what we are able to provide at a given time. Does that mean if you give forty-percent instead of ninety-percent you are a failure? Absolutely not! So long as you give that forty-percent your best effort. This really is all about you!

Claudia was in charge of the decorations for an event at her Women's Group. She was scheduled to get everything completed the afternoon before the function. With a detailed vision for the atmosphere she wanted to create for the event, she could hardly wait to bring her ideas to life. One day before she was supposed to decorate, she came down with the flu. Her attempts to get someone to fill in for her were futile with such short notice. As she dragged herself out of bed to get ready to go to the conference room to decorate, she knew her original ideas would have to be scaled down because there was no way she had enough energy to get it all done. She finished the job in just over four hours, and as she looked around she sighed because she had so wanted to put the lavish decorating scheme into place, but had to give herself a huge pat on the back because despite how lousy she felt, the room looked darned good! She decided not to scrap her original ideas for the room, but to try to incorporate them into their next scheduled event.

Claudia knew she was not capable of putting the elaborate decoration scheme together while she was sick, but she did not consider it a failure. She was proud of herself. She did the best she could and that was all she was able to do.

We need to take our cues from within. If we are true to ourselves and in touch with our feelings, we will always be in

a place where we can do our best. Our best, not the best that others can do, or what others think we should do. It is very important to remember this. If we forget it we are acting from a place of "should" and that is a road better not traveled at all.

Coach's Corner

Is there anything you've done recently you feel is less than your best? How do you feel about it? Be honest, especially if you're still beating yourself up for not doing as good a job as you're capable. Remember when Thomas Edison's lab burned down, his comment was, "Thank goodness all our mistakes are gone. Now we can start over."

What mistakes do you want to burn to the ground so you can focus on doing your best in this moment?

Step Out of Your Comfort Zone

Yes, it is important to have down time. And, yes, it is very important to do your best, even when you are feeling tired or low. But, did you realize most of the limits we place on how effective we can be are self-imposed limits that can be easily stretched?

We are a learning society. We spend many years and countless hours learning things in school, taking refresher courses, pursuing post-graduate level course work, and Internet classes. Yet, when someone does not succeed, it is a truly enlightened individual who remembers to label it for what it is ... a learning experience. People who are able to recognize this when it shows up in their own lives are able to use it to their advantage. In fact, they are typically very successful because they possess a "willingness to fail." They are able to look at what most would consider a failure as a means to get to their final destination. Just because they go off track temporarily does not mean they are not closer to their target. It is simply targeting, realigning, and targeting again until whatever they are after is achieved.

> *"There are many who fear the unknown. It's important to remember the unknown is full of adventure that will surprise and delight you."*
> ~Eva

It is often said children can be cruel, but it is adults who are cruel. Adults would never look at a young child attempting something and label that child a failure. They would say "Aww, Sally that's okay, that was a good try, you'll get it next time!" They might even remark to another adult that it's so wonderful to see how far Sally has come over the past few weeks. As adults, we forget that life is a constant growth process. We are always capable of learning no matter how old we are, and we should continue to take risks. We should never be fearful of failure because failure is just another form of constructive learning. Why is it constructive? Because failure that fosters lessons and growth is constructive. It is in alignment with the Universe, and positive self-talk is the best way to approach our endeavors.

If fear of failure is keeping you from attempting something you long to do, ask yourself why you are letting it worry you. Isn't taking a chance by doing something much more courageous than doing nothing at all? If everyone thought of failure as a major obstacle, we would not have the technological advancements we are currently so accustomed to. How many times did Sir Isaac Newton have to be bonked on the head before he made sense of the Law of Gravity? What about Benjamin Franklin and his kite, or scientists and their cures and vaccines? The point is we would still be in the Dark Ages if various inventors, scientists, and others had refused to step out of their comfort zones and dare to take a chance at failure. Isn't it time you made your mark?

Failure is just one step in the right direction to the ultimate goal of growth and success. Don't be afraid to try new things, stretch beyond your comfortable limits, and stray off course. The worse that can happen is you'll fail, learn from that instance, and get to try something new.

Coach's Corner

Dust off those roller blades, go take that snowboarding lesson, or sign up for that class. Life is too short to play it safe all the time. Go fail ... er, I mean learn!

What is it you have been wanting to do, but have not because of fear? Identify one step you can take towards making it happen and do it this week.

Choose Your Path

*D*o you wish you could do something over, take back an action, or exchange an utterance? The bad news is you can't. What's done is done. The good news is it's already in the past and this is the first moment of the rest of your life. As much as you might personally abhor that cliché, it just so happens that it is true. Since you can't change the past, what does your future hold? It's up to you to choose.

As a society we are often stuck in a rut; not satisfied with our past and our present, but reluctant to step up to the plate and make the future what we desire. Too often this occurs because we don't realize we created the path we are on consciously or unconsciously. But nothing is written in stone. Change begins first with a thought, followed by a choice, which becomes an action.

Jenny was very depressed. It seemed no matter how hard she tried she couldn't get her business off the ground and her bills were mounting to epic proportions. She knew if she couldn't turn things around relatively quickly she would soon be facing bankruptcy. Knowing things were out of hand she asked her best friend to lunch for some advice. Over lunch, Danni listened attentively as Jenny got her up to speed. When Jenny was done, Danni took a deep breath and said, "So, what are you choosing to do about it?" Jenny stopped chewing and thought about how Danni had phrased the question and asked her what she meant. Danni proceeded to explain to Jenny in detail, just how much control she had over her situation.

First, she asked Jenny to describe her thoughts about her

business and her finances. Jenny told Danni having her own business had always been a dream of hers, but she never had enough funds coming in, her client list was pitifully short, and she was rapidly losing hope. Once Danni understood Jenny's feelings she asked her to describe her ideal situation. As she watched, Jenny's face became animated, her voice became passionate, and her eyes lit up as she described oodles of serious fun clients, fulfilling projects, and an abundance of funds. When she stopped speaking, Danni asked Jenny to focus on her "success vision", to choose and embrace it as her reality, to think about it at least three times each day in great detail and to let go of the thoughts that had landed her in her situation. Lastly, Danni suggested Jenny monitor her progress each day by acknowledging the changes in her circumstances with some form of appreciation. When Jenny did not respond Danni gave her examples of things to appreciate, like a new client, a potential referral, free advertising. Jenny decided she had nothing to lose, so she decided to give it a try.

About three months later Jenny called Danni and asked her to come over for dinner. When Danni arrived she found a beautiful table set, with a cake that had two words on it - Thank You. Jenny explained she had spent the past three months showing appreciation for everyone and everything that showed up, but Danni deserved something extra special for helping her turn her life around. Jenny told Danni her business seemed to take off within two weeks of their conversation. She had new clients, changed her marketing materials, and had even been approved for a loan she had forgotten she'd applied for. Jenny's business was becoming successful, and she was positive it was because she stopped playing the martyr and decided to choose to be successful.

Coach's Corner

Are there things in your life you would like to release? Or things you would like to see materialize? Are you ready to make the choice to be what you want? I'd like you to close your eyes and visualize your dream life. If it's different from the life you have, then you have a choice to make. Simply becoming aware of the thoughts you hold and changing them to appreciation will have a profound affect on your life. Don't worry about what has already happened. Remember, this is the first moment of the rest of your life.

Empower Yourself for Success Today!

*Y*ou understand your past is done and you get to choose what happens next, right? Have you taken the time to visualize your dream life? If you haven't, I suggest taking a moment to do exactly that right now, before you proceed.

Ready?

Do you know you have the power to succeed at everything you do right now? Are you surprised? Your thoughts control the actions that create your successes or failures. So if your thoughts are the foundation for success, if you spend some time focusing on the type of thoughts that are typically manifested and the ones that create success, you'll have the tools necessary for self-empowerment.

When it's time to try something new do you run right out and jump into it, confident you are going to succeed with no doubts? Isn't that a wonderful picture? Unfortunately much of the population first has to contend with a little negative self-talk, a personal "gremlin", if you will. Are you familiar with the gremlin? Perhaps you know him or her by a different name. He or she sits waiting to shoot down our ideas, deflate our elation, and sabotage our plans ... when we allow it to happen.

Often, this negativity is so common we don't even recognize it when it is occurring, therefore, we are unable to stop it. So, when we carry on with our activities we are often full of doubt, harboring feelings of incompetence, and brandishing insecurities that are setting us up for failure, or at the very least a much more difficult road towards success. The worse case scenario is when we allow our gremlins to stop us from even trying to reach our goal. So how do we silence the gremlin, and replace it with our own personal cheerleader instead? There are several ways.

> *"You may not be able to change everything, but you can't change anything unless you're willing to look at it."*
> ~Eva

Learn to recognize the gremlin for what it is. It is a thief that stifles creativity, hinders success, and paralyzes growth. Then, begin to listen carefully for that voice and cut it off before its effects can take root. Remember that idea about wearing a rubber band on your wrist? Do this for a month and give yourself a "zing" whenever you hear that gremlin beginning to discourage you. Talk about a reminder! I don't know about you, but I'd rather zing the gremlin than myself any day!

Surround yourself with positive, happy people who do not allow gremlins to steal their successes. It becomes very difficult to continuously hear about positive things without some of your own to add. You'll start looking for ways to join the crowd.

The more you are around positive thoughts, the more real they become, and the more you attract the same back to you.

Coach's Corner

Recall the times when you successfully combated your gremlin and let those serve as your road map. Knowing that you have what it takes to face any challenges and overcome your obstacles, is just the thing needed to bolster your confidence and self-esteem - two of the things that gremlins seem to sap out of their victims. Don't be a victim any longer, be a victor.

Lastly, write them down in your journal. Journaling is a wonderful way to chronicle your victories. Writing things down allows you to explore the feelings, thoughts, and circumstances that surrounded the experience. Details that are typically glossed over could be extremely beneficial when later explored.

So are you ready to step up to the challenge? I know you can do it! Learning how to silence your gremlin is a tool that will be beneficial for life. Isn't it time to empower yourself and position yourself to succeed at all you set out to accomplish? Yes, Yes, and YES!!! Put your cheerleader to work today!

Learn Life's Lessons

*H*ave you learned from the lessons that everyday life has tossed out? I'll bet those annoying gremlins aren't bothering you as much as they used to because by now, I suspect, you look at what life has to offer as challenges, and approach them as opportunities. If this is true of you, I also would wager you do learn from your experiences.

If on the other hand you are more apt to place blame on yourself or others, use excuses to explain a circumstance, or prefer to be a spectator in life, then you are probably missing out on some awesome opportunities!

I know we cannot accept the blame for everything that occurs in life. But, just because you can't accept the blame does not mean you can assign it to someone else. Why give them the control over a situation? Things happen, but it is up to each of us to use these things to our advantage whenever possible and take charge of our lives. It is our responsibility to use whatever tools are at our disposal to achieve the goals we set, no matter the obstacle.

> ***Getting up when you've failed
> is a victory."**
> ~Eva

Meet Sam. Sam has led a tough life. She left home at a young age, lived on the streets, yet she still managed to make the most of her life. She went to college, earned several degrees, and has a successful career in banking. Sam did learn the lessons of life, and paid attention ... unlike Andrew. Andrew also did not have an easy time of it while he was growing up, but instead of allowing his circum-

stances to fuel his desire to achieve and succeed, he allowed them to be limiting. He focused on how rough his young life was, how unfairly he was treated, and how much he was owed due to his wronged past. Needless to say, Andrew has not found success. In fact, just when things look like they are about to turn around for him, Andrew's attitude becomes a weapon of self-sabotage. Andrew has thoroughly mastered the art of laying blame, but not the lesson of accepting responsibility for oneself. Andrew, for now, seems quite comfortable living his life at the ends of a puppeteers strings instead of controlling his own destiny. So are you a Sam or an Andrew?

How do you react to the things life dishes out? If you find yourself wondering how you made it to this point in your life, or questioning how to get to a different point, just ask yourself if you've been the driver or the passenger thus far. There is a saying that, "there is no such thing as an accident." I believe the things that occur in life do not just happen. We have the power to control our lives by accepting responsibility for what shows up, and using each experience as a learning tool. Reach for the throttle and more success will follow. I'll leave you with just one piece of advice for now: V-ROOM!

One of the things that happens when you let go of blame and take full responsibility for your life is you'll naturally attract people who want to help you. It is a truly remarkable experience when allowed to take place. In the next chapter, I'll show you how you can accelerate this process by consciously and deliberately creating your own dream team!

Coach's Corner

What's one thing that has happened to you in the recent past? Who are you blaming for this?

I want you to decide that you're letting go of blame, right now! If you were to accept complete responsibility for everything that happens from this point forward, what would that mean? What actions will you take? How will you feel? Right now, start acting *as if* you have complete responsibility, even if it doesn't feel quite right yet.

CHAPTER 8

Building Your Attraction Dream Team

"I know my place in the Universe more and more clearly as I live from my authentic self. In doing so, I become
a catalyst for others to live from their authenticity.
And by recognizing my uniqueness,
I allow the uniqueness of others. At that point, there is
no room for competitiveness or
exclusion." -- Eva

Uncovering the Essence of You

*I*n life, as you go about your daily tasks it is so easy to lose sight of a very fundamental important fact: you are your most important resource. Your ideas, skills, qualities, and characteristics - the essence of you - are what will propel you toward success, or hinder your progress if you allow it to. Which will become your reality?

> *"You can influence yourself into your greatness by seeing yourself having reached your potential. And you can influence others into their greatness by doing the same for them."*
> ~Eva

As you go about building your own Attraction Dream Team, remember that this team all starts with you and what you have to offer. Do you remember making a Pluses-versus-Minuses, Good-versus-Bad chart? Well, it's time to dig out the pen and paper or fire up the computer. Your chart will have one side marked "Advantages" and the other marked "Disadvantages". Your Advantages column will contain all of the assets you bring to the table. The Disadvantages column will contain all of the liabilities. Please remember to be realistic, thorough, and above all, honest. While it may be eye-opening, and perhaps even a little unflattering, to see "you" listed on a legal pad or on a computer screen, this may be just the catalyst needed to implement change. These changes are the adjustments necessary to shorten your liabilities column and lengthen your assets tally.

The charting exercise is a tool that will help you move towards success at a more rapid rate. Always keep the goal of success in the back of your mind. When you think about the qualities that are your assets, consider whether or not these have really helped you to create success in your life.

> *"Mutual respect and understanding allow*
> *relationships to grow and flourish."*
> ~Eva

For example, Gerald is a well-educated man in his mid-thirties. He has always taken pride in the fact that he made his own way in life. He got himself into college on an almost-full scholarship, paid his way by working two jobs while in school, and has even managed to pay back the bulk of his student loans. He did this all without asking anyone for any assistance.

Is this an asset or a liability? We are taught that being self-sufficient is an admirable trait, but in his quest for success and prosperity, Gerald's trait could be a serious liability. Gerald's reluctance to seek the help of others could be extremely detrimental to his success, since we know that we cannot be all things, solve all things, or foresee all things. The way to increase the probability of success is by combining the assets of everyone on a team.

Gerald's is just one instance of a characteristic that is strong in one area. This strength could have a different set of repercussions when applied to a different scenario. So, when you are sitting down to make your list of Advantages and Disadvantages, hold the intention for yourself that the list you generate will be for the sole purpose of success and prosperity. Without the creativity behind the thought that sparks the idea, nothing would come to fruition. The creativity begins with   Y-O-U. It's time to uncover, explore, and celebrate the assets that are the essence of you and give credit where credit is due.

Coach's Corner

Go ahead. Pull out your journal and create your list. One side is Advantages (assets) and the other side is Disadvantages (liabilities). Examine each item you place on each side from the perspective of success and prosperity. Will this particular characteristic move you toward success, or impede your success? Will it help you achieve prosperity or keep you in relative poverty? Be honest with yourself so you'll know which characteristics you want to emphasize, and which you want to no longer give attention to.

Choose Your Friends Wisely

ou're not the only one on your dream team, of course. As individuals concerned about quality of life and the environment, I am sure that you frequently consider how the environment affects your well-being. Asking questions about what is being spewed into the air that is breathed, dumped into the water that is drunk, or absorbed into the food that is eaten, has become commonplace. What about your social environment? It has just as much of an impact on your life, and in most cases, the effects are more readily felt than those of, what we consider, the outside environment.

> *"Who do you find yourself surrounded by? The people in your life are a reflection of the type of person you are. If you are surrounded by joyful folks, it is a reflection of you. If you are surrounded by less than joyful folks, it is a reflection of you. In order to be with those in joy, you must first be joyful yourself."*
> ~Eva

The people that interact with you on a daily basis -- friends, colleagues, significant-others and family members all play principal roles in your life. While it is impossible to choose all of your colleagues (even if you own your own business), and you definitely cannot choose your family members (as much as we may wish, on occasion), you can choose your friends and significant-others (as they typically start out as friends first). Look at those people you consider friends. Do you honestly feel like you have built a community of supportive, fulfilling relationships? Or does your list of friends resemble a patchwork quilt because the relationships just developed and were not nurtured or deliberately created.

Now I hear you thinking, "I like my friends. Why would I want to deliberately look for friends, anyway?" The answer is, because the type of people you spend time with is a direct reflection of who you are, what you feel, and what you do. If you hang out with people that are always broke, never happy or satisfied, constantly complaining, or always playing the victim, their situations will affect you. How can their situations be reflected in your life? If you are a true friend you will at least feel sad for your friend and it will make you sad. In other situations, you can actually find their emotions, beliefs, and actions being reflected in your life as well. Tim can illustrate this point nicely.

Tim has had the same group of three friends since high school. They are all twenty-five years old, but Tim is currently the only one of them that is employed. He is an assistant manager at a sporting goods store. He often hears his friends complain about the lack of opportunity because of the state of the economy, how unfair life is because you cannot get ahead without a college education. And, even with a college degree, the job market is saturated. They even complain about how they can never find decent dates. Tim had been considering returning to college but changed his mind right before the start of the new semester. His girlfriend was so upset that she broke up with him and told him he was never going to get ahead if he continued to associate with his "loser" friends. Tim now has the chance to become manager of his store. Want to bet his friends will find some way to put a negative spin on it for him? Tim is clearly being affected by the attitudes and beliefs of his friends. In fact, they are the epitome of negativity and have adversely impacted his life.

"I decided I wanted to let go of direct contact with negative people, including family and so-called friends. E-mail is a great way to stay in touch without the negative influence of their tone of voice, mood, etc. It's a lot easier to dump negative people, too.

More importantly, I needed and wanted to let my business and social friends and family "in" more. I found that, somehow, I was not letting them past a certain safe point for me.

An example of this is how I went to events that weren't interesting or rewarding for me simply because I was expected to go.

I've shifted that, and this lets everyone in on how I'm really feeling, which makes our relationships more positive."
~Mary

If Tim had put careful thought and emphasis into choosing his friends, his scenario may actually look quite different. For example, Tim and his girlfriend meet his friends after work. He tells them that he is being considered for a promotion, but he has a problem because he is also attending school. They brainstorm a bit, realizing this is a fantastic opportunity for him and come up with a brilliant plan. They suggest Tim contact the school and see if his work experience could be applied towards college credit and then meet with his regional manager to determine if he would be willing to mentor Tim as a co-op student. What a difference! The type of people Tim considers as friends has dramatically changed the course of his life with a single interaction. Imagine the affect this could have over a number of years!

Chapter Eight: *Building Your Attraction Dream Team*

"I allow in my community only those that are supportive of my dreams and me. By this, I mean that I share my dreams with only those that say, "You go, girl!" I no longer associate with people that believe that destiny is already written, that the world is a scary place, or they think the most times life is a path of suffering and struggle.

I am not saying that I only associate with Pollyanna, but I let in my community only those that can have a bad day, still expect the best of life, and believe that joy and abundance are our right. They believe that dreams do come true and life is good.

My family, whom I adore, may not always fit this description, but most of the time I am able to know this for them even when they don't know it for themselves. I let go of my lunches with coworkers. I maintain personal contact with the people I love from the church, but I chose not to be part of a group anymore. I do not need to that an more, unless it is positive and rewarding."
~Annabelle

How does one build a community of fulfilling relationships? Begin by looking for people that share things in common with you, or possess those qualities you would like to nurture within yourself. People that have similar interests, hobbies, lifestyles, goals, or personalities are a great place to start. Once you begin meeting people, evaluate how they react to their environment. If you react similarly, or you find their reaction positive, I dare say you might have a winner. If you do this a few times, you will find yourself surrounded with like-minded people you will feel truly connected with.

"If life is a dance then friends are the music."
~Eva

There is nothing wrong with looking to maximize the number of positive interactions that can occur each day. If you and your friends can nurture each other and improve the quality of each others' lives, only good things can come of this. How many times during childhood and adolescence did you hear you should "choose your friends wisely?" Imagine that! The adults actually knew what they were talking about after all!

Coach's Corner

Get out your journal and make a list of all your friendships. Look at each one closely. Is this person a positive or negative influence on you and your life? Do they promote your well-being and success, or insist that you join them in misery and poverty?

Does this person align with your values and what you believe? Or, do they promote something quite different?

Make a decision about your friendships. Which do you want to nurture because you will grow and be nurtured, and which do you want to move away from? These are difficult decisions, but in the long run you'll be extremely thankful. Those who want to join you in your positive, abundant place will do so of their own choosing.

Create a Mastermind

*N*ow it is time to be really deliberate about your dream team. Napoleon Hill says that, "power may be defined as organized and intelligently directed knowledge." By "organized" he refers to an organized effort produced through the coordination or effort of two or more people who work toward a definite end, "in the spirit of harmony."

He also defines the Mastermind as "coordination of knowledge and effort, in a spirit of harmony, between two or more people, for the attainment of a definite purpose."

With me so far? I'm talking about a group of people who you gather around you for the sole purpose of your success and prosperity – a mastermind that is far greater than any of the individual members. Remember how the Laws of Attraction work? Well, double, triple, or multiply that by 10 times when you gather around you a group for the attainment of a definite purpose – your purpose.

> *"Those who hold big dreams with integrity attract*
> *others that catch the vision."*
> ~Eva

What does a mastermind group do?

A mastermind group typically consists of up to eight people who brainstorm with each other, give and receive feedback, share best practices, and hold each other accountable for following through with their commitments. They also share their goals, success stories and setbacks. Sound good? I hope so!

One person in each mastermind group usually is responsible each meeting to act as facilitator or chairperson. This person sets the agenda, coordinates schedules and logistics. The leader role rotates for each meeting, so everyone gets a chance to lead.

I think the biggest benefit of a mastermind group is the power of accountability and commitment. When a group of people put their positive thoughts and energy behind me, I feel a surge of energy to accomplish what I've said I'll do. We all demand the best from each other, and because we fully support each other's growth and well-being, we're all more likely to take some risks. You can get referrals, feedback, business or emotional resources, or any number of things from your mastermind group.

Here are some tips for creating your own mastermind group:

1. Enlist five to eight of your trustworthy, creative and successful business friends. Be creative and selective in your choices. You want people who are positive, creative, open, and know that their success depends greatly on your success.
Coaching/Feedback for each person – 40 minutes

Closing, set agenda/place for next meeting/call – 5 minutes

If your agenda calls for a specific topic for discussion, allow for enough time, and end the discussion at the designated time, even if someone gets "cut off". Everyone makes a commitment to begin and end on time. This creates an element of trust and helps maintain positive energy in the group.

If possible, don't cancel a meeting. Attempt to reschedule, and have the meeting even if someone is missing.

Establish a consistent meeting environment. Perhaps you'll have snacks, or a short break. This depends on the length of your meeting and the areas in which you'll focus.

Make sure the time is shared equally! Some people are naturally more talkative and can dominate a meeting. This isn't helpful to anyone.

Ask everyone to come prepared to the meeting with their homework complete if possible, and an idea of what they'd like from the group in this meeting.

Have some way to plan and track each meeting. Have a time keeper and a scribe who records action items each person agrees to take before the next meeting. These notes are distributed to each member within the week.

Once you've got your mastermind in place, your friends and associates fully behind you, and your own inner self in alignment, you're ready to really make things happen. In the next chapter, I'll give you some ideas for so totally accelerating your use of the Laws of Attraction that you'll feel like you're going at warp speed. ZOOM!

2.   It helps to have some diversity in your group. If you all think exactly alike, you won't learn much!

3.   Schedule regular meetings or calls, whether they're weekly, monthly or quarterly. It doesn't matter where or how you meet, only that the group does meet regularly.

4.   Create a mission statement for the group. Set your intentions and vision, as you would for yourself. The same

keys to success outlined in this book apply to a mastermind group.

5.   Close your group once you get your core membership. You need to build trust, and this takes time. Make all meetings completely confidential. What's discussed in the meetings stays in the meetings.

6.   Establish clear ground rules for the group – what you will and won't do. Set standards of behavior that you hold each member to. What are grounds for dismissal from the group?

What to do at a meeting:

Have a clear agenda for each meeting and stick to it. An agenda can be as simple as:

Set intentions for meeting or call – 5 minutes
Individual check-in from last week – 10 minutes

Coach's Corner

Who do you want in your mastermind? See if you can come up with at least three names, then have each of those three add one more person. This keeps the group diverse, and quickly gets you up to seven people, a good number for starting out.

Decide ahead of time the purpose of your mastermind. Is it Prosperity? Investing? Building a business? Decide what will serve you the best, then choose three people you would love to share this journey with you. And, of course, have fun!

CHAPTER 9

Zoom ... Accelerating Attraction

"Our thoughts are like tiny drops of water.
One drop may be fragile and easily blown around.
Yet, just as the force of a tidal wave or flood forms
when enough drops combine, the thoughts we keep
thinking over time become an unstoppable force.
Enough thoughts focused on a subject, a desire or an
outcome guarantee its manifestation." – Eva

Unleash Your Creativity

We live in a hectic time. Ours is an instant gratification society. We want it now. Yet, as we reflect on the best things in our lives, we often find the truly important things (like relationships, love and peace) took time to develop.

The 'always on' nature of the tools we use in business can all too easily trap us into believing that we can function as machines too.

> *"The music of the Universe consistently plays in the key of joy - your joy."*
> ~Eva

But we're not machines, we're human beings.

Is there a way to achieve peak performance and happiness in life too? Of course.

Here are five factors which, when practiced consistently in your life, will help you tap into the giant creativity reservoir you have within.

1. **Find your peak mental time.** You may hear some people say "I'm a morning person" while others say they don't really get started until 11 pm. There is no right or wrong in these situations, but it is vital to know who you are and go with that rather than fighting it. One great way to discover your peak time is to keep a log of how you feel. Keep a log for a week, noting when you felt the sharpest. Then arrange your work around these peak hours, planning the most important tasks for this time. Many have found once they harmonize with who they really are, they get much

more done in less time.

2. **Make a 'creativity appointment' with yourself.** Plan thirty minutes every day during this peak time for a "creativity appointment." Make this time as undisturbed as possible. Use this time to connect deeply with your mission in life.

3. **Get ready to solve a problem.** During this time, think deeply for the first ten minutes about the biggest problem you face. Allow yourself to play 'what if' about the challenge you face. If you had every resource a person could have, would it still be a problem? What if you tackled it and did nothing else? Would that solve it? What if you neglected it completely for two weeks? Would that make it worse, or make it go away?

4. **Let your subconscious work.** After these ten minutes, and for the rest of the time, let your mind wander anywhere it wants to go. If possible, look outside and look at the sky. Even better, go outside and listen to the sounds of nature. You want to think expansively now, to consider all possibilities.

5. **Prepare for the answer.** During this quiet time, keep a pad and pen handy and write down any new and creative thoughts that come to you. You may find that during this time new, and very exciting, thoughts and possibilities rush into your mind. Write each one down, no matter how silly they may seem.

Be consistent. The more often you keep your creativity appointments, the more you will find that you have the "aha!" moments during your day, when solutions to problems just pop into your mind.

"When things really started to take off for me, I real-
ized that I was relaxed ... that was always my
biggest desire. I stepped into trust more solidly...
I made a choice and now I talk to the Universe
quite often!"
~Jeanna

Expand the appointments to include a half-day a month and you will unleash even more creativity. Soon, you will hunger for these times because you will find it is while doing nothing at all that something very good gets done.

Coach's Corner

Ready to give this process a try? Pick something small at first so you can get the hang of the process. What's a rather small "problem" you're facing?

Follow the five steps as described on the previous pages.

What ideas did you come up with? Did you have fun? Was it exciting to try this out? Yes? Cool! No? See if you can try an even smaller problem so that you'll be relaxed about it. Once you see it work, you'll be able to trust and tackle larger problems.

CHAPTER NINE: *Zoom ... Accelerating Attraction*

Close Your Eyes and Dream!

*Y*our creativity is a very powerful force – one that helps you to achieve amazing things. Your imagination is equally powerful! Dreams cannot harm you; instead, they can help you immensely. Not the ones you have when you're sleeping, but the ones you hold in your heart - your fondest desires. Those dreams can shape your reality if you take the time to give them life and to visualize them. Do you ever wonder about the self-confidence that successful people always seem to have? It's that self-confidence that got them where they wanted to be. They focused on the goal – their *big dream* - and the mind and body made it happen.

> *"You move fastest through transition*
> *when you don't try to rush it.*
> *There is great learning at every stage."*
> ~Eva

Do you ever play "what if"? Sometimes playing "what if?" can be very effective if it puts you into a state of feeling good. However, sometimes it can cause you to spiral downward. So, instead of playing "what if", why not play "I am".

How does one play? It all comes back to be-ing. You can be what you want if you can picture yourself being it, living it, and experiencing it. Close your eyes, relax, and imagine that you are the successful _____, and that you live in the beautiful _____, overlooking _____. You have a wonderful life. You are able to relax and enjoy life to the fullest. You are content and all of your worries are gone. Use all five of your senses.

"When things really started to accelerate for me, I realized I had a total commitment to manifest my desire, all day, everyday. I was dedicated to vibrating to match my desire.

Meditation has been an invaluable tool. As the mother of a toddler, I found it difficult to meditate daily. But meditation on a daily basis accelerated the manifestation.

What I am doing now is bringing the meditation techniques to my daily life like bringing up feelings of joy periodically using pictures posted in my computer desktop, or the picture of my son - something to constantly remind me of how joyful my life is."
~Annabelle

Elaborate from this initial "I am" picture. What kind of house do you live in? Where is it located? Is this your summer home? What does the air smell like when you arrive at your home? Is it by the sea? Is it in the country?

Can you see it clearly? How does it make you feel? Do you feel like it is really yours? Do you feel as though you've earned it, that you deserve all that you are visualizing? This too is part of the process. When your feelings are one with your thoughts and beliefs, and they are focused on the positive goals that you have set, the picture you are holding in your mind's eye will begin manifesting. In essence, you've used your thoughts to attract the people, ideas, situations, and events that will bring you the vision you are holding of yourself, thus creating your reality.

Bridget was feeling exceptionally low when a friend suggested she schedule a session with a personal coach. She was hesitant and skeptical, thinking there was not anything her coach could tell her she hadn't already thought of, envisioned, or dreamed of herself. She found she was both right and wrong in her assumptions. When she met Dora she was impressed by how grounded she was and by how much they had in common. She also found out a couple of years before Dora discovered coaching, she was feeling adrift and had a business that was floundering. Bridget readily identified with this because her gift shop had been doing so poorly lately, that she had a number of creditors calling looking for payment. Dora told her she used visualization to obtain her goals. Bridget scoffed at the idea. But when Dora explained that someone told her if she could not visualize herself as a success she would never be a success, it began to make sense. Bridget didn't think she thought of herself as a failure, but realized she also did not think of herself as a success.

> *"When you begin focusing on how you are feeling,*
> *rather than what you are thinking, you begin to*
> *attract what you want. The Universe is responding*
> *to how you feel."*
> ~Eva

Bridget spent fifteen minutes twice a day visualizing herself running a successful business, living in the house of her dreams and living a debt free life. After a few weeks, she noticed the change in the level of confidence she had in her abilities. She approached her business dealings with more self-confidence, which in turn began to increase her bottom line. Her increase in confidence made her much more attentive to her customers which produced larger sales. With Dora as her coach, Bridget used her dreams to obtain her reality. She visualized, imagined, spoke about and wrote down her goals to support her state of being. She refused to back down and allow limiting thoughts to tarnish her future.

Coach's Corner

If Bridget could do it, so can you! Let go of the limiting thoughts and begin by embracing the life you want, desire, and deserve. Let the picture you see in your mind support your goals and you will help them materialize that much faster. Let your dreams be the guide to your future and the road to your success. You just have to close your eyes and ... *dream*. Try this for fifteen minutes twice each day, and see how you begin feeling about yourself and your ability to attract what you want.

Learning to Think Powerfully, Like the Masters

*I*f you really want to accelerate your success, you can begin by believing and thinking the way the masters believe and think. Yes, they tap into their creativity and their imaginations. But, they do much more.

One of the things many successful people have in common is confidence. They have the confidence they will achieve the things they set out to, they will get all they feel entitled to, or they will create the things they desire. They do not allow doubt or negativity to sabotage their plans. Most have become masters at focusing on the positive and refuse to let the "little voice" within feed them negativity for them to buy into. So how have they mastered the power of positive thinking or even more difficult, the skill of positive self-talk?

> *"Commitment is what transforms
> promise into reality."*
> ~Eva

Perhaps you should first listen to the things you tell yourself on a daily basis. Do you realize how true the saying "we are our own worse critic" is? Try this. Close your eyes and listen to the message your self-talk is delivering. Are you happy with what you are hearing? If not, why not try implementing some of the hints outlined below.

Write down five of the things you catch your self-talk telling you. For each negative thing you write down, change the tone to make it a positive by using "I am," "I will," and "I can" instead. Be sure to make these affirmations positive, believable, and realistic for you personally. Now *feel* what it is like to have it actually be the way you want it to be. Get excited about the possibility. Build on the affirmations that create a story about how it all unfolds the way you intend for it to often, and in time, you will come to believe them. The more you believe the positive, the more success you will have. You will begin to attract it -- literally!

"As I got more in alignment with what I was wanting to create, I got rid (and am still getting rid of) lots of unneeded stuff - both physical things and thoughts that are old and need to be discarded.

As I've done this, my ability to manifest what I've wanted has increased. I'm attracting more and better things and a feeling of ease....actually a kind of constant feeling of closure. This keeps me in integrity with my beliefs, ethics and values."
~Mary

While evaluating your self-talk, did you discover you spend a great deal of time thinking in "What-ifs"? Remember me mentioning this in the last chapter? What-ifs are typically a big waste of time because you spend valuable time focusing on things that have either already taken place, or may or may not happen. What if (sorry -- couldn't resist) I show you how to make What-ifs productive?

Every time you find yourself focused on negative thoughts or a default reaction of "What if....?" Play the "What If-UP Game!" This is a highly successful game I use with my coaching clients. It goes like this:

Whenever you start thinking **"What If ..."**

- **What if** I can't meet payroll?
- **What if** I can't pay my bills?
- **What if** I can't complete this task?

Flip the thought around to:
- **What if** it could be the way I want it?
- **What if** I meet payroll in spite of the way things look in the moment?
- **What if** money begins to flow to me and I can pay my bills the way that I want?
- **What if** this task gets completed in perfect timing even if it isn't what I thought it would be?

See how it works? The game is designed to get you thinking about the positive and letting go of the negative. Using the word "could" eliminates self-imposed pressure and opens the door to unlimited possibilities.

> *"You draw to you what you do want through your*
> *positive emotions. The more intense the emotions,*
> *the more quickly it comes to you."*
> ~Eva

The key to positive thought and self-talk is recognizing what you are currently doing and learning to deliberately change it. Once it is learned, it will have a profound impact on the things you would like to accomplish in life. As William Shakespeare once said, "Nothing is good or bad, but thinking makes it so." So, think of this as the first day of the rest of your life and start thinking powerfully and putting out a positive attitude in each aspect of your life.

✑ *Coach's Corner*

What if ... everything you thought and did from this moment on was positive and enhanced your success and prosperity?

What if ... you now had all the knowledge, wisdom, and resources to achieve your wildest dreams?

What if ... you were powerful beyond measure and there was really nothing, but your own mind, that could stop you?

What if ... Hmm?

The Secret to Making it B-I-G

With all these tools and ideas at your disposal, how could you possibly still be thinking small? How about starting to dream big, using all your faculties to imagine you can obtain your wildest, biggest, seemingly impossible dream? Now that you've imagined it, have you asked yourself how to get it? If not, that could be what is halting your forward progress.

> *"The more sensitive you are to your emotional state, the more guidance you can receive from your inner wisdom. The emotion that you feel will let you know. Positive emotion is an indication that you are in alignment with your inner intentions. Negative emotion is an indication that you are not."*
> ~Eva

The mind is a wonderful thing. It works day and night to solve the things that are presented to it. In fact, it won't stop until we acknowledge that the result is to our liking. How often have you pushed something out of your consciousness only to have it resurface in your dreams? That's the mind still working on the solution that was requested.

Since questions predetermine answers, the problem that most of the population faces is they dream too small. How often have you found yourself asking for a new job, a 5% raise, or a couple of new clients? While you have effectively mastered asking and manifesting your requests, what if you began asking bigger questions, like "how do I become a millionaire?" In other words, think, dream, and question big! Imagine putting the mind to work on that one!

Joel sat by the water staring ahead but not seeing the glorious view or appreciating the beautiful day. Instead he was buried in distress. He had just a few days to come up with the money to pay his bills and he was horribly short. So he sat by the water trying to think of ways to secure the much needed cash. Borrowing the money was out. Overtime would provide the funds, but not in time. While he was contemplating his dilemma, an older gentleman of about 70 sat down at the other end of the bench. After a few moments he asked Joel why he had such a heavy heart. Joel replied that his finances were strained month after month, and this month was the worse yet.

The older gentleman looked at Joel for several seconds and replied, "So, what are you going to do about it?" To this Joel snapped "Well, if I knew that, I wouldn't be sitting here!" The older gentleman thought for a moment and said "I think that you have finally found the problem." To this Joel looked at him with exasperation clearly etched on his face.

> *"The more emotion behind a thought, the faster its physical manifestation - whether the thoughts and emotions are positive or negative. Once you understand that, you understand how you've created the life you are living."*
> ~Eva

The older gentleman drew a deep breath and began to explain it slowly. "You see, young fella, you have spent so much time dwelling on how to meet your monthly obligations, that you have not spent any time trying to solve your lifetime obligations. I don't mean the financial obligations to others, but the ones you owe to yourself. So, I suggest that you broaden your line of sight and try to determine how you're going to make your success for one year, ten years, twenty years, and finally a lifetime. Don't fret, ask the questions and the answers will come. In the meanwhile you'll find your daily, weekly and monthly expenses will take care of themselves."

The older gentleman got up from the bench, placed his hat on his head, tipped it to Joel and carefully made his way back down the path. At the end of the path Joel saw a chauffeur waiting patiently for the gentleman, with the door held wide. Joel looked after him for a few minutes and decided then and there to put the advice given to him to use. He figured he had nothing to lose, and the old gentleman must know a bit about what he suggested if he could afford a chauffeur-driven limousine.

Are you going to take the advice of the old gentleman too, and broaden your line of sight? Are you asking the BIG questions and letting the little ones fall into place on their own? Let your mind do what it does best and solve the problems for you. Just remember that you asked the question, so be on the lookout for the answer when it comes. Please note the verbiage - *when* it comes, not *if*, for the answer will come.

Whew! It has been fabulous riding this huge wave of attraction with you! Ready to finish it all off with a little topping of sweetness? Well, in the next chapter, we'll do just that! It has indeed been a pleasure!

Coach's Corner

What is your BIG question? Ask it now... Okay. Got it?
Write it down in your journal.

Now, make it a little bigger. Imagine that you're blowing
up a balloon, and you're afraid it will pop. What's the bigger question? Write that question in your journal.

Now imagine that this balloon is made of a special material that is unbreakable. How big will you blow your balloon? Continue writing the bigger question until you've
exhausted possibilities.

Now go ahead and ask yourself the **bigger** question. Now
let your subconscious go to work finding the answer for
you. Be aware of any inspired ideas that come to you and
act on them!

CHAPTER 10

Putting It All Together

"I thought I was here to change the world. I found I was
here to change myself." --Eva

What's Your State of Mind?

*D*o you question the notion that there is enough abundance to go around – for everyone? Why is that? Is it because we have been conditioned to believe that only a select few will reach the personal and financial goals to which they aspire? Or because we have bought into the saying that "if something seems too good to be true, it is", and believing that abundance abounds would certainly seem too good to be true.

What if abundance began and ended with you ... with your thoughts, your beliefs, and your actions? Would you be more apt to embrace the belief? Ironically, the abundance that shows up in your life, or the lack of it, is directly correlated to you and your beliefs.

Abundance is everywhere. Like Niagara Falls, in its natural state it is a constant flow, plentiful, only diminishing when tampered with.

Abundance follows the same principle. It exists for everyone that keeps an open mind and does not diminish the flow. Besides Niagara Falls, can you think of another example of abundance? What about the air we breathe? Or perhaps the choices that are ours to make? Both of these abound.

If abundance seems to be missing in your life, what is your current state of mind? Are you addressing all the things you would like to have but do not? If so, you are perpetuating lack and pushing abundance further from your reality. In *The One Minute Millionaire*, Mark Victor Hansen and Robert G. Allen provide an exercise designed to help

change your state of mind to one of abundance. They suggest that it be done twice a day, just before going to sleep and getting out of bed each morning.

"It is kind of like a roller coaster when things are moving quickly. Then just when I need to take a breath - it slows down and gives me the rest I need to take on the next adventure.

I've been able to create for myself more time, money and loving people around just when they were needed and wanted. I have less worry and am living by the simple phrase, "I AM HAPPY".

This is a life skill, and life still happens around us...and you can still get back on track if you realize that TRUTH WILL WIN OUT."

Blessings,
Mary

The four statements should not just be repeated, but should be said with belief and conviction:

I am abundant in every good way.

Infinite money is mine to earn, save, invest, exponentially multiply, and share.

My abundance is making everyone better off.

I embrace abundance and abundance embraces me.

Do you feel the power emanating from these statements? Do you believe them? If you are finding it difficult to accept

them, give it time, but continue on with the exercise. It generally takes three to four weeks for a repetitive action to become a habit, and for a belief to gel. In time the affirmations will become your reality and you will find yourself recognizing abundance all around you.

Can you think of people who have abundance showing up on a regular basis? What do they do to have this always present in their lives? There are many admired celebrities that live the principle of abundance. Take Oprah, for example. One of the wealthiest women in the world who has made the commitment to give back - The Angel Network, The Book Club, and bringing to the forefront things that can help everyone create better lives for themselves and those around them. Oprah has embraced abundance, and clearly she continues to magnetize it. Can we take a life lesson from her? Should we? YES!

Stop buying into the "not enough" principle. There is enough ... more than enough for all of us. It may just take a little effort on your part to change your state of mind from lack to abundance. Don't you think it's worth it?

Coach's Corner

If you're still sitting on the fence, take out a sheet of paper and write down the things that have been showing up thus far, and the things you believe will show when you start practicing the Laws of Attraction. Just so you know, you will run out of paper as your list will have an infinite number of possibilities that have been just waiting to flow from the tip of your pen. What an awesome habit to pick up, the habit of embracing abundance.

Soar to Freedom

Can you feel it? The freedom to live life as you choose? To make decisions based on your desires instead of necessity? The opportunity to live life to the fullest and experience all of the things you thought were out of reach? Does this sound too good to be true? It's not!

Freedom is available to you at any time ... even now. When you decide to pursue a lifestyle full of freedom, you make a commitment to be successful in your life dealings to W-I-N at all your endeavors. Like everything, it begins with you.

The ability to attract wealth is the starting gun in the freedom race. Why wealth? Because while money does not guarantee happiness, it does pave the way over the bumps that cause many to stumble. It helps eliminate the stress and worry associated with bills and debt, and takes away the "shoulds" and "musts" that accompany thoughts of lack.

"I always get what I want, when I don't focus too
intensely on it. Things come on a different time
frame than I usually expect and I've learned that it's
okay. Nothing will fall apart in the meantime. Enjoy
now. Trust. Send some cool clients my way. Tell
Oprah to get Eva and me on her show."
~Jeanna

What follows wealth? The freedom of time. Does just the thought make you sigh? Imagine the time to do what you would like to do, not what you feel pressured to do. To

have the time to pursue a hobby, spend unlimited amounts of time with your loved ones, or to go on a trip or for a walk for the sheer enjoyment of the experience? To have the chance to pursue your passions because you no longer come from a place of not enough money or time? Are you beginning to feel the energy of freedom? Intoxicating, isn't it?

Next there is health. While good health is vital to the pursuit of freedom, without money to ease stress and time to put good healthful practices into place, the ability to achieve the best possible health is often impossible. Would you enjoy the freedom to have a home gym and the time to devote to training for a marathon? Or the ability to schedule childcare for a session with a personal trainer or to hire a dietary nutritionist for meal planning and cooking lessons. Health freedom, when coupled with wealth and time is the most valuable form of freedom there is. To have the freedom to do the best that you can for yourself for the rest of your life, and to help those around you do the same.

"To bring all the answers to a conclusion I would say this is what works for me:

I chose an idea of what I want my life to be. I identify the ME that I want to be, and this may come in different forms. Maybe it will be represented in a desire for a house, a mate, or even a car. But it is the idea of "the ideal me" I want to be. That's what I identify first.

Then I allow myself to believe that it's possible for me to experience, be or have this. I start playing with how I would feel if ... I become familiar with the feeling, I bring it closer to me every time.

*I visualize, I daydream, I find pictures, and songs
that help me stay focused on what I want.*

*My vision becomes closer to me than my hands and
feet, closer to me than my own breath. I become the
vision, in a dream in a moment of unbelievable joy
(for no specific reason) and in that holy instant the
creation of my dream has begun. When I feel that
joy, sometimes in just a second, I know I can rest, it
is done and I go about my business of the present
moment.*

*Hope this helps your millions of readers to bring
their dreams into their physical reality."*
~Annabelle

What about spirituality? How about having all the time to
explore your beliefs, pursue them and integrate them into
your life? Beliefs, no matter what they are, are important.
It's one of the things that many never have time to pursue
due to daily demands and pressures. Something that lives
in hearts, but is not allowed to blossom outside of the person. Wouldn't it be wonderful to be able to embrace and
unleash your spirit too?

When one has the freedom of wealth, time, health and spirituality, one has what can best be described as ultimate
freedom. What does this term mean to you? Close your
eyes and imagine a life with all of these freedoms already
present. Can you feel it and embrace it? Are ideas for new
projects, experiences, and concepts bursting forth? Are
visions of happy faces and feelings of contentment filling
your heart? Ultimate freedom provides you with all of the
core tools necessary to propel you towards your passion
and destiny.

Coach's Corner

Make the commitment today. Put the Laws of Attraction to work and take the first step towards wealth, time, health and spirituality with ultimate freedom being your eventual goal. It's not elusive at all. You can soar to freedom!

Resource Guide

*T*he following is a list of recommended books, courses and services in alignment with The Feel Good
Guide to Prosperity.

<u>Recommended Services</u>

Abundance Abounds
Portal site to all products and services by Eva Gregory
www.abundanceabounds.com

Leading Edge Coaching and Training
Individual coaching, teleclasses, seminars, workshops and
keynote speaking
www.leadingedgecoaching.com

Partner4Success Graphic design
Creative designs for web sites, books, and more by Susan
Johnson
www.partner4success.com

The Writer Dude
Ghostwriting, copywriting, critiquing services and personal coaching using the Laws of Attraction by Sid Smith.
www.writerdude.com

Just Write 4 You
Resumes, copyrighting and ghostwriting by Kim Green-
Spangler
www.justwrite4u.com

Recommended Courses

The Prosperity Game by Eva Gregory and Jeanna
Gabellini
www.theprosperitygame.com

The Magnetizing Money System Home Study Course by
Eva Gregory, Jeanna Gabellini, Sharon Wilson and Terri
Levine
www.magnetizingmoney.com

Recommended Web Sites:

**The Feel Good Guide To Prosperity
Official book web site
www.feelgoodguidetoprosperity.com**

Abundance Abounds
Portal site to all products and services by Eva Gregory
www.abundanceabounds.com

Abraham-Hicks
Official site for all Abraham-Hicks works
www.abraham-hicks.com

Recommended Film

What the Bleep Do We Know, by Lord of the Films, LLC,
2004
www.whatthebleep.com

Recommended Music

Scott Johnson, Googol Press
Music to Transform Your Life
www.googolpress.com

Recommended Reading

Leading Edge Living: Taking Your Life From Ordinary to Extraordinary
F*R*E*E* e-zine by Eva Gregory
Send an email to Eva@LeadingEdgeCoaching.com with Subscribe in the subject line.

Ask And It Is Given by Jerry and Esther Hicks
Carlsbad, California: Hay House, 2004

Attracting Perfect Customers, by Stacey Hall & Jan Brogniez
San Francisco, California: Berrett-Koehler Publishers, Inc., 2001

Effortless Prosperity by Bijan
Las Vegas, Nevada: Effortless Prosperity, Inc., Second printing, 1998

Law of Attraction by Michael Losier
Victoria, BC Canada: Michael J. Losier

Messages From Water by Masuro Emoto
Japan: Beyond Words Publishing, 2004

One Minute Millionaire by Mark Victor Hansen and Robert G. Allen
New York, New York: Harmony Books, 2002

Power vs. Force by David Hawkins
Carlsbad, California: Hay House, 2002

Spiritual Marketing by Joe Vitale
Bloomington, Indiana: 1stBooks, 2002

Think and Grow Rich by Napolean Hill
N. Hollywood, California: Wilshire Book Company,
Reprinted 1999

You Were Born Rich by Bob Proctor
Cartersville, Georgia: LifeSuccess Productions, 1997

Are You Ready for More?

Please contact Leading Edge for more information on classes, programs, books and audio programs by Eva Gregory. Be sure to visit our web sites often for a variety of programs, keynotes, workshops, seminars, teleclasses, and products to help you in attaining a prosperous life.

Leading Edge Coaching and Training
Phone: 510.597.0687
Fax: 510.588.5477
Email: info@leadingedgecoaching.com

Web sites:
www.abundanceabounds.com
www.evagregory.com
www.feelgoodguidetoprosperity.com
www.jeannaandevashow.com
www.leadingedgecoaching.com
www.magnetizingmoney.com
www.milliondollarmarch.com
www.theprosperitygame.com

Look for The Feel Good Guide to Prosperity in the following formats:
   Hardback
   Paperback
   E-book (pdf download)
   Audio
   MP3 download

To join our mailing list, email your name, email address, full mailing address and phone number to info@leadingedgecoaching.com with FGG MAILING LIST in the subject line or call toll free 510.597.0687.

We do not sell or share your mailing information with third parties.

Printed in the United States
23766LVS00001B/28-33